River Cottage Baby & Toddler Cookbook

River Cottage Baby & Toddler Cookbook

Nikki Duffy

**Foreword by
Hugh Fearnley-Whittingstall**

Photography by Georgia Glynn Smith

B L O O M S B U R Y

LONDON · NEW DELHI · NEW YORK · SYDNEY

1. STARTING OFF

2. RECIPES

FOREWORD
by Hugh Fearnley-Whittingstall

FOR MORE than twenty years, I've had a consuming interest in food: where it comes from, how it's grown or reared, and how it is prepared. I'm as passionate about a delicious dish on a plate as the next greedy person, but I'm interested in the whole story of what we eat, from first principles.

This passion took on a new focus eleven years ago when our son Oscar was born. When, at five months old, he started to take an interest in solid food, I was conscious that this was about more than just nourishment; this was the beginning of Oscar's lifelong adventure with food. Of course we dabbled with baby rice, and the odd organic rusk. But we really didn't see the need to unscrew any jars. Oscar was born in early March, and his first forays into the world of solid food coincided with the late July/early August boom in the River Cottage veg garden. It was hardly a chore to mash up a bit of the veg that we were devouring ourselves and offer it up to Oscar on a spoon or a bread soldier.

So Oscar was weaned straight onto mashed carrots, bashed beetroot, creamed spinach, crushed courgettes and puréed peas, shortly followed – as autumn then winter came – by endless variations on the multi-root mash theme, not to mention compotes of our own apples, pears and plums. We'd often give him a little of whatever we were eating too – fresh fish, meaty stews, even curries – provided it was of reasonably gum-friendly texture (Oscar was in no hurry to grow teeth). It was an enormous pleasure seeing him enjoying the produce Marie and I had grown ourselves, and effectively sharing our meals with us.

Early on, we tried to broaden Oscar's interest in food. Marie and I took him out into the garden in his sling as we picked tomatoes or courgettes, or pulled up the carrots. Back in the kitchen he sat in his chair watching us cook, pottering about, peeling spuds, pulling something out of the oven, prodding, stirring and tasting. Not that it was intended to be a show for his benefit. We spend a lot of time in the kitchen, so where else would he be?

But nonetheless we hoped that Oscar – and all our children – would realise from the beginning that the kitchen is an exciting place to be. It's where the action is. It's a cliché to say that the kitchen is the heart of the home, but it's a cliché I'm rather fond of repeating. It's also a playground, laboratory, mission control. It's where the good stuff happens.

Of course, it's not always easy. There's nothing quite so humbling as presenting a bowl of lovingly prepared veg to the child you've lovingly reared and seeing it used as an adornment for hair, clothes, floor and wall. Any smug feelings are soon banished as you witness the carrot stick or broccoli sprig, so popular only last week, being vociferously rejected. It's easy to say be relaxed about it, but it can sometimes be frustrating and stressful.

And that's where this book, or more precisely, Nikki Duffy comes in, dispensing encouragement, good sense, wisdom and delicious, everyday recipes. She has also, in the course of researching this book, spoken to many parents. So the advice and recipes here reflect a wide range of experiences – from joyful and thrilling to maddening and completely blooming baffling.

I first met Nikki when she commissioned me to write a feature for a magazine she was working on. She impressed me with her intense interest in food and where it comes from, her knowledge and calm good humour. Eventually – knowing a good thing when I see it – I persuaded her to come and work with us at River Cottage. At that point she'd just had her daughter Tara and she later went on to have Edie. And just recently Marie and I have added little Louisa to our brood. So during the course of our friendship, we've spent plenty of time talking about babies and children and their exciting, intriguing and, at times, perplexing journey with food.

Nikki's approach is based, as it should be, on capturing a baby's natural enthusiasm and curiosity for food, but she knows that's rarely as straightforward as it sounds. So her pragmatic mixture of awareness, ingenuity (bordering on cunning) and optimistic persistence is both inspiring and trouble-shooting. With Louisa, encouraged by Nikki's brilliant chapter on weaning, we have been following a more hands-on approach (her little hands, not ours) with great success. Veering towards 'baby-led' weaning, which Nikki explains with great clarity, we have learned to tolerate a fair degree of mess for the sheer joy of watching Louisa feed herself, with a surprising degree of competence and good

judgement. She's not a stranger to the spoon and the purée (she loves
a tart apple compote) but they probably only feature once a day.

I've read other books brimming with tactical and nutritional advice
on feeding your little ones, but Nikki conveys an important message: that
feeding time can give you quality family time; that sharing and openness
around food, which make family mealtimes such a joy, can be introduced
right from the off; that there's no real need to feed anything (except
mother's milk) to your baby that you wouldn't happily eat yourself or feed
to the rest of the family – even if in slightly chunkier form.

There's no hectoring here. No lectures. Just lots of hard-won information
and advice. Both Nikki and I believe that good nutrition – for young and
not so young – is not about becoming obsessed with what to avoid, so much
as celebrating all of the delicious foods you can embrace enthusiastically.
I'm sure that her terrific recipes for everything from porridge and smoothies
to soups, pâtés, burgers, pies, risottos and stir-fries, jellies and crumbles,
will soon become favourites in your house as they have in ours. Just make
sure you cook enough for everybody. And serve the youngest first.

Hugh Fearnley-Whittingstall
February 2011

INTRODUCTION

AS A PARENT, there are few things so good, so utterly satisfying as seeing your child enjoy a meal you have cooked for them. The pleasure is all the greater when you know the food you've given them is wholesome, nutritious and carefully prepared. The pursuit of this joy, the fulfilment that comes from providing well for the people you love, is at the heart of this book. More than the precise balancing of different nutrients, more than perfect presentation, more than persuading them to eat what you want them to eat, I think feeding children well should be about instilling a love of good food and of shared eating.

That, however, is not always easy. Unless you're blessed with very pliant offspring (if you consider that a blessing), you will likely, at some point, come into conflict with them where food is concerned. If not, you will probably at least have to wrestle with your own concerns over exactly what they're eating – how much of this and how much of that, how it's been cooked, where it's come from.

Feeding small children can sometimes be difficult, frustrating and anxiety-inducing. And no one can take that anxiety away: like so many aspects of parenting, you have to work through it yourself because no matter how many times other people tell you it will turn out all right, you never really know that it will turn out all right until it actually does. However, I hope I might be able to lessen the stress a little. Because there are lessons I have learned, and lessons learned by the many parents I have interviewed, that are worth knowing about.

If you take only one message away from this book, I hope it's this: try to relax. We all have varying experiences of feeding our children but almost every parent I have spoken to, when asked what they might do differently next time, said they would endeavour to worry less and relax more about exactly what, when and how their child eats. The parents who most relish and enjoy the time they spend eating together with their children are the ones who are reasonably laid-back, from the very first solid food onwards.

That's not to say that you do not need to think about the quality of the food you give your children. Of course, you should aim to serve up delicious, health-enhancing meals, but I don't think that's very difficult. You don't require a degree in nutrition to get a pretty good feeling for what's good for them and what's not – just basic info and a bit of common sense. And this ties into the other really important thing I want to pass on, which is that we, as parents, need to trust ourselves.

When it comes to raising our children, we are robbed of much of our self-confidence these days. Medical professionals, child-rearing experts and even well-meaning friends and relatives can all bombard us with advice that makes us doubt our own instincts. There's nothing wrong with doing research and getting plenty of information, but don't underestimate the importance of your own feelings when it comes to deciding the best way to feed your kids. And don't underestimate their feelings either – all children have different needs and different appetites, as well as strong instincts about how much they need to eat. It is very much research and info, rather than rules and dictates, that I'm trying to present in this book.

I am not a scientist or a doctor or a nutritionist. I'm a mother, a cook and a writer. In putting this book together, I've done a huge amount of research and spent many hours consulting with Frances Robson, a wonderful paediatric dietitian, and numerous other knowledgeable sources. But, for myself, I can claim to be an expert only on my own children. You are the expert on yours.

When you accept this, and when you make a decision to simply do the very best that you can, I think you are well on the way to the right destination. Mealtimes with young children can be a challenging part of parenthood, but they can also be a source of immense joy, fun and satisfaction. When a meal is a truly communal experience, something a family enjoys together – the food, the conversation, even the tidying up – you are all enriched by it in an emotional as well as a physical sense. For me, that's what it's all about.

1. STARTING OFF

Raw Ingredients

The food you choose for your kids

IT'S A CLICHÉ but it's true: we all want the best for our children. I'm sure you, like me, and just about every other parent in the world, want to offer your family the highest quality food possible. But quality isn't just about how fresh and flavourful and delicious your ingredients are, it's also about how your food has been produced, where it's come from, what impact it's had on the environment. That's why, before I even begin to talk about how you approach feeding your kids, I'd like to consider how we can all go about choosing ingredients which are really great, in every sense of the word.

This is a River Cottage book, so I'm sure you won't be surprised to find me championing the use of locally grown, seasonal fruit and veg, and organic or free-range dairy products and meat. Neither will it shock you to discover that I think it's best to cook most of your family's food yourself, from scratch. I feel passionately about this approach and there are very good arguments for doing things this way.

However, as the parent of a young child just embarking on the great adventure of eating, I know the last thing you need is something new to worry about. I don't think anyone would expect you to stick rigidly to principles of only local, only seasonal, or only home-made foods when you're negotiating the early days of feeding. I certainly didn't. Like me, you'll probably be guided to some extent by what is appropriate and desirable for your baby to eat, what they actually like, and what is convenient for you to buy and prepare.

But do look at this time as an amazing opportunity to explore good food – especially food that's grown near to where you live – and to sample it in a very pure and unadulterated state. In short, take pleasure and pride in giving your child the very best you can.

'When my first son was born, I could barely boil water and he had quite a lot of convenience baby food. But by the time my second son came along, I'd taught myself to cook. I made all his food from scratch using organic ingredients. The difference in my boys' eating habits now is remarkable. I strongly believe those early days have formed their appetites.'
Sonrisa, mum to Aaron, 13 and George, 10

'Having children has changed the way I cook. Now I cook more than I did – in fact, I feel I'm planning, shopping or cooking all the time! I now buy organic fruit, veg and meat as far as possible. I don't buy pre-prepared stuff because I want to be in control.'
Becky, mum to Isabel, 3, and Jasmin, 7 months

'We have to make sure one of us has the time each evening to actually cook a meal. Or we set aside a Sunday afternoon to make bread or a batch of soup. It takes time but it's also relaxing, and it makes a really big difference to how we all eat. We save work by always cooking too much of things and freezing some, and we do a menu plan every week.'
Mark, dad to Nell, 3

Why Cook?

Take a look at the baby food section of any supermarket and you will be presented with an amazing range of gorgeously packaged, utterly delicious-sounding, pre-prepared foods that need no more preparation than removing the lid or opening the box.

A lot of these ready-made baby foods are organic, low-sugar, salt-free, preservative-free and nutritionally balanced. Some are no more processed than a carton of natural yoghurt or a jar of nut butter and, of course, they are awfully convenient. Why wouldn't you buy them? Actually, I don't think there's anything wrong with giving your child good-quality food from a jar or a packet sometimes. I just think it's better to cook things yourself, from scratch, most of the time – and this is why:

- Home-made food tastes better. I can't claim to have eaten my way through every commercial baby food on the market, but I've tasted a few. And I've found them bland and sludgy at best, and really quite unpleasant at worst. A jar of pasteurised 'chicken casserole' purée is a world away from some fresh, home-cooked chicken and vegetables chopped by hand or whizzed in a blender.

- Making your own food means you are in charge – you are the quality controller, you judge the freshness and taste of the ingredients, you know exactly what's gone into the food and exactly what hasn't.

- Home-made food is cheaper because you are paying only for raw ingredients, not manufacturing, packaging and marketing.

- It's much easier to offer your child food based on local, seasonal ingredients if you make it yourself. Many pre-packed baby foods are manufactured overseas.

- Nutritional content is affected by many factors, but home-prepared food cooked from fresh ingredients has the potential to be more nutritious than commercially prepared food that's stored in a packet or jar.

- Every time you buy a packet of baby food risotto or fruit porridge, it will taste exactly the same. Every time you make a risotto or a bowl of fruit porridge, it will taste slightly different. Variety, even at the most subtle level, is crucial in helping your child accept a balanced diet.

- If you cook for the family as a whole, your baby or toddler will be eating the same kinds of things you eat, and sharing meals with you – both of which are incredibly important in establishing good eating habits.

- When your child watches you cooking with fresh ingredients, or putting something home-made on the table, they learn that this is normal and desirable. Even when they are too young to join in themselves, they will begin to learn something about cooking just by seeing you do it.

- Commercially prepared foods generally involve more packaging.

- Cooking is a lovely, creative, therapeutic thing to do. In a day filled with the frustrations and demands of childcare, housekeeping, work – whatever your particular lifestyle dictates – cooking food for the family can bring valuable focus, fulfilment and pleasure. I know that it can be difficult to find time for cooking when you have small children. But I also know that preparing their food yourself brings a deep satisfaction that cannot be overlooked.

Food Shopping

Eating seasonally and locally has a particular relevance when you are feeding small children because not only do ingredients tend to taste better, they can be better for you. Food produced nearby can be picked when it's ripe and ready and full of flavour. It should be fresh as it doesn't have to be transported far and very fresh food is more nutritious than food which has been stored. The vitamin content of fruits and vegetables decreases rapidly after picking (see page 24). At the end of this chapter, you'll find a guide to seasonal British fruit and vegetables, and some ideas for the best ways to use them.

Where you shop

Buying locally produced food usually – though not always – involves using a local retailer. Small independent butchers, fishmongers and greengrocers, farm shops, box schemes, farmers' markets and roadside stalls can all be excellent sources of local, seasonal fare. And such small-scale retail often provides a much more immediate sense of where food has come from, how it was grown and its seasonality, which is fantastic if you take your children shopping with you. You don't have to live in the countryside to buy local food – many farmers' markets take place in city centres and many box schemes deliver in urban areas.

While shopping locally may be a burgeoning trend, most of us still buy a lot of our food and drink at supermarkets. Of course, they are convenient and offer a lot of choice. Sometimes they can even be a better alternative, supplying something that your local farm shop doesn't, perhaps, such as sustainably caught fish, British rhubarb or unsalted butter. So, while I think we should all be supporting local retailers, I am certainly not against supermarkets. I just think it's important to use them, not be used by them.

Mail order food buying is another option for busy families and has many advantages, particularly if you have small children who don't seem to enjoy browsing in shops. You can find pretty much anything you want from specialist mail order suppliers. The downsides are the food miles and the packaging. The latter can be excessive, particularly if you're buying chilled foods. So, use the internet and supermarket home-delivery services to source the ingredients you can't find nearby, or to save the day when the household is ravaged by chickenpox, but don't rely on them to the exclusion of other retailers closer to home.

Organics

Whether food that is produced organically has a higher nutritional content remains a matter of debate. But for me, the amount of vitamin C in an organic carrot compared to a non-organic one is far from being the whole point. There is convincing evidence that organic food can be beneficial to health in other ways. Levels of salmonella are lower in organic egg-laying hens than others, for instance, while studies have shown that additives found in some non-organic foods can increase the risk of hyperactivity in children (more on this later).

It's also a fact that a lot of non-organic food, particularly fruit and veg, contains residues of pesticides. Washing or peeling fruit and veg removes pesticide residues in some cases, but not all. There's little definitive research on the long-term effects of consuming pesticides, or the amounts that should be considered harmful, but some are potential carcinogens and some are potential hormone disruptors. It's worth noting that, whatever the effects of consuming pesticides in food may be, children will be more vulnerable. For a start, their exposure is greater because they eat more in proportion to their body weight than an adult does. And there's also concern that their immature systems may be less able to deal with and eliminate toxins.

Fruit and veg certified as organic have been grown without artificial fertilisers and using far fewer pesticides than conventional produce. High standards of animal welfare must be met and organic farmers do not use antibiotics routinely. They also often work in a way that is respectful of, and more beneficial to the natural environment. A lot of parents choose organic food for their children for these reasons – not as a guarantee of perfect health, but because they want to reduce the amount of chemicals they consume and live in a greener way.

I never specify organic ingredients in recipes because I think it's up to the individual to make choices like that, but I use a lot of them myself.

Buying meat, eggs and dairy products

I think it's important to exercise good judgment whenever you buy a food that has an animal as its source – whether it's the animal itself (meat), or a product (eggs, milk, yoghurt, cheese etc). You are probably familiar with many of the ethical arguments for choosing higher welfare meat, eggs and dairy products (there are many excellent sources, including *The River Cottage Meat Book*, that can fill you in if you're not). However, you might not be aware that organic, free-range and grass-fed animals can produce meat, milk and eggs containing higher levels of some desirable fatty acids and antioxidants, as compared to intensively farmed ones. For me, choosing 'higher welfare' options, such as organic eggs or meat from outdoor-raised animals, isn't just about ethics, it's about more nutritious food. I choose organic meat, dairy and eggs if possible – local too, if I can.

If organic is not available, look for the 'higher welfare' options:

- Free-range British chicken and eggs, rather than intensively farmed ones.

- Outdoor-reared or free-range British pork, rather than intensively farmed, indoor-reared pork.

- British rose veal, rather than 'white' veal from Europe, where welfare standards are lower.

- Beef from small British producers, ideally from traditional beef breeds such as Aberdeen Angus or Hereford, grass-fed and outdoor-reared.

- Lamb (or hogget or mutton, which are one- or two-year old sheep) from small British producers, grass-fed and outdoor-reared.

- Wild game such as venison or rabbit.

Buying fish

Fish is a wonderful food for children: a fantastic source of protein and other nutrients such as iron and those crucial omega-3 fatty acids. But it is also one of our most abused resources and shopping for it can sometimes seem like a minefield. The advice on buying individual fish species changes frequently and the area the fish comes from determines how 'ethical' it is. North Sea cod stocks are heavily depleted, for instance, but you can buy cod from the north-east Arctic which is certified as sustainable by the MSC.

Fortunately, there are many organisations and retailers now working to make responsibly sourced fish available and easily identifiable. Use facilities such as fishonline.org (the Marine Conservation Society's consumer site) to gain a clear idea of species that are plentiful and areas that are well managed. Choose, if you can, fish with the Marine Stewardship Council's certified-sustainable logo. For what and where to buy, see msc.org.

Try to find out how the fish was caught. The more selective the fishing method, the better. Avoid trawled fish as this method isn't selective, and can damage the sea bed; 'line-caught' is preferable as the seabed is untouched. Hand-line-caught is an even more selective method. 'Pole and line', 'hand-line' or 'troll-caught' are the most sustainable options for tinned tuna. Choosing fish caught from small day boats is another sound decision as the fish are likely to have been caught in small numbers. If buying farmed fish, go for organic. Organic aquaculture has a lower environmental impact and the fish are treated with fewer medicines and chemicals.

A summary of current advice relating to fish used in the recipes:

- When it comes to chunky white fish, coley, pouting, pollack and gurnard are all pretty safe bets, line-caught Cornish sea bass likewise. If you fancy cod, choose MSC-certified Pacific cod (from Alaska), or line-caught cod from the north-east Arctic. The most sustainable haddock is from the north-east Arctic, again preferably line-caught.

- For oily fish, line-caught mackerel is generally a good choice – ideally MSC-certified. Wild salmon stocks are under severe threat in many areas so try to find MSC-certified wild Pacific salmon (again, from Alaska), or organically farmed Atlantic salmon (usually Scottish).

- If you're buying prawns, choose cold-water or northern ones. The status of cold-water prawn stocks is uncertain, so I use them judiciously; I add a few from time to time to chowders or fish pies. I never buy warm-water prawns such as tropical, king or tiger prawns: wild ones are trawled unsustainably, and farmed ones can be produced in dreadful conditions.

Buying fresh fruit and veg

It doesn't matter if you're in a supermarket or an organic farm shop, you still need to make decisions about quality each time you buy fresh produce. When you're buying fruit and veg, look, smell, have a gentle prod. There's nothing wrong with the odd blemish or peculiar shape, but avoid anything that looks bruised, damaged, wilted, under- or over-ripe, and anything that doesn't smell good – wrinkled apples, yellowing broccoli and bendy carrots are no good, not even if they're local. Not only will they be uninspiring to eat, their nutritional content will be reduced too. Being choosy may mean you can't always get what you went out for, but many recipes can easily be adapted to use different fruit or veg. And, when you do find something fresh and inexpensive, buy lots of it! Never mind one bagful of plums, get three or four! Buying and cooking in bulk is a key way to make the most of seasonal ingredients. Having things stashed away in the freezer saves you time and, crucially, it saves you mental effort.

Preserving Nutrients

Some nutrients can be significantly affected by storage and cooking. Vitamin C is the obvious one, but all water-soluble vitamins are vulnerable, including vitamins B6, B12, biotin, folic acid, niacin, pantothenic acid, riboflavin and thiamin. These are mostly found in fruit, vegetables and grains. In all cases, levels decrease as a food is stored, if it's exposed to air and light (by chopping, for example) and if it's put in water and/or cooked.

To get the most vitamins from fruit and veg, we really need to eat them very fresh, and raw. However, where that's not feasible, there are other ways to maximise the vitamin content. Consider frozen vegetables: as these are often frozen soon after picking, the vitamins are preserved. If you can, prepare food just before cooking, rather than leaving it sliced or chopped on a board or in a pan of water. Keep the skin on (not always appropriate with young babies, granted). Try steaming instead of boiling (less vitamin-leaching into the water) and, if you cook veg in water, use the water in gravy, stock or soup. And remember that even when cooked, fruit and veg still retain useful quantities of vitamins – and other nutrients.

There are plenty of nutrients that are not affected, or at least not very much, by cooking or by storage. These include the fat-soluble vitamins A, D, E and K and also calcium and iron. There are even some nutrients which are more available from cooked food – we absorb antioxidants better from tomatoes and carrots when they are cooked, for instance.

Storing and preparing fresh fruit and veg

While fruit and vegetables will lose some nutritional value in storage, they won't lose all of it, and there are some which will stay good for some time if kept in the fridge or in a cool, dry cupboard or larder. Root veg, apples, squashes and pumpkins all fall into this category. Other fresh produce, such as berries, sweetcorn, peas and asparagus, will deteriorate relatively quickly, so eat them as soon as you can, or consider ways to preserve them. It's much better to freeze your freshly podded peas, or make soup with that glut of tomatoes, for example, than leave them sitting about in their raw state losing condition.

To help you make the most of British fruit and veg, the chart on the following pages gives a rough guide to seasons, optimal storing strategies and uses. Do remember to wash fruit and veg well before serving it to your family – to remove residues, chemical or natural.

Food	In season	Storage	Got a glut?	Recipes
Apples	August–March Look for different varieties through the season	In a cool, dry room, away from direct sun, for weeks	Purée (see page 105) and freeze in portions. Use grated in coleslaw, cakes or burgers, or chopped in salads.	Pages 108, 112, 113, 114, 142, 172, 175, 195, 200, 203, 219, 220, 234
Apricots	July–August	In a cool room or the fridge, for a few days	Purée. Freeze in portions (see page 105), or mix with yoghurt.	
Asparagus	May–June	In the fridge for a day or two, but loses flavour all the while	Try blanching spears, then roasting, griddling or barbecuing. Excellent with eggs. Makes lovely soup. Use cooked spears as finger food for babies.	Page 124
Beans, Runner and French	July–September	In the fridge for 2–3 days	Cooked till tender, these make good finger foods. Slice, blanch and freeze for later cooking with garlic, herbs and cream. Or cook with a tomato sauce (see page 212); freeze in batches.	Pages 204, 210
Beetroot	July–December	In a cool room for a week or so, or in the fridge for up to 2 weeks	Roast and skin (see page 109), then use chopped, sliced, grated, or puréed – in salads, soups, dips, risottos, stews, even cakes. Cut into fat fingers for babies. Use leafy beetroot tops like chard (page 126).	Pages 109, 177, 203
Blackberries	July–September	In a cool room for 1–2 days, or in the fridge for 3–4 days	Open-freeze, then pack in a tub. Add to muffins, crumbles and pies. Purée, sieve and combine with cooked apple (see page 113).	Pages 113, 142, 192
Blueberries	July–September	In a cool room for 1–2 days, or in the fridge for 3–4 days	Open-freeze, then pack in a tub. Add to fruit salads, yoghurt, pancakes, muffins, smoothies.	Pages 113, 146, 192
Broad beans 1kg pods yields about 300g beans	June–August	In the fridge for a day or two, but they lose sweetness all the while	Pod, blanch, skin and freeze ready to add to pasta, risotto, frittata etc. Or cook and crush with garlicky butter, or use to make houmous (see page 245) or soup.	Page 245

Food	In season	Storage	Got a glut?	Recipes
Broccoli (calabrese)	July–September	In the fridge for a few days	Steam, purée (see page 105) and freeze in portions. Steamed florets are ideal first finger food. Also great with pasta, in frittatas or tarts, or in salads. Good with dips.	Pages 108, 122, 124, 132, 161, 162, 204
Brussels sprouts and Brussels tops	October–March	In the fridge for up to a week	Finely slice and stir-fry sprouts, or give them the cauliflower cheese treatment. Leafy tops are a good alternative to cabbage or spring greens.	Page 207
Cabbage, Spring greens and Kale	All year round, depending on variety	In the fridge for a few days	Remove tough stalks and shred finely. Add to pasta to cook, drain and toss with gently fried onion and grated cheese. Also great combined with fried, mashed or roast potatoes. Try in a mixed purée (see page 111). Finely chop and add to egg dishes.	Pages 111, 120, 180, 203
Carrots	Available all year Small, sweet new season carrots start in May	In a cool room for a week, or the fridge for 2–3 weeks	Grate and add to salads and slaws, or cakes and muffins. Always keep some handy for making soup and stock (see pages 236–8). Fantastic roasted, or in stir-fries, stews, purées.	Pages 106, 108, 175, 179, 191, 203, 209, 210, 214, 218
Cauliflower	Available all year	In the fridge for a few days	Purée (see page 105) and freeze in portions. Good in soup, curry or cauliflower cheese. Or steam, cool and toss in a light dressing, or try raw, with a dip.	Pages 108, 119, 177, 207
Celeriac	September–March	In a cool room or the fridge for up to 2 weeks	Combine with potato in gratins, mash or purées, or with other root veg for roasting.	Pages 106, 111, 201
Celery	September–January	In the fridge for up to 2 weeks	Essential for stock (see pages 236–8). Try thinly sliced and tossed with grated cheese, or braise in chicken stock. Leaves are good in salads.	Pages 119, 139, 141, 175, 177, 179, 191, 214, 218, 238

Food	In season	Storage	Got a glut?	Recipes
Chard (Swiss, rainbow, ruby)	August–November	In the fridge for a couple of days (will quickly go floppy)	Separate stems and leaves. Chop and stir-fry stems first, then add the sliced leaves. Great in tarts, on pizza, in frittatas and pasta sauces.	Page 126
Cherries	July–August	In a cool room for several days	Try halved and stoned in puds or pies. Or stew gently to make a compote. Never give to small children without removing stone first.	Page 192
Courgettes	July–October	In the fridge for a few days	Slice thinly, sauté in a little butter or oil until soft and crushable. Use as a pasta sauce or freeze. Add to tomato sauces and risottos.	Pages 152, 154, 161, 162
Cucumber	July–October	In the fridge for up to a week	Blend with yoghurt and crushed garlic to make a cooling summer soup. Lovely in salads with olives. Good cut into sticks as a finger food.	Page 186
Currants (black, white and red)	July–August	In the fridge for up to 2 days	Open-freeze, then pack in a tub. Blackcurrants need sweetening – good puréed and folded with cream or yoghurt and custard. Red and white currants can be eaten raw (could be a choking risk for babies). Try in salads, sweet and savoury.	
Fennel	July–October	In the fridge for a few days	Delicious raw in salads or for dipping. Fantastic roasted, or in a gratin. Makes good soup. Sauté with garlic, add a little crème fraîche and serve with pasta.	Pages 177, 186, 188
Gooseberries	June–July	In the fridge for a few days	Open-freeze, then pack in a tub when raw, or cook with a little sugar and water. Delicious combined with strawberries or apples (which may negate the need for sugar). Some varieties are sweet enough to eat raw.	Page 170

Food	In season	Storage	Got a glut?	Recipes
Jerusalem artichokes	November–March	In a cool room or the fridge for up to 2 weeks	Peel, then boil or roast. Good combined with other mashed or roasted roots. Can be eaten raw, finely sliced or grated.	
Leeks	September–April	In a cool room or the fridge for a few days	Slice, wash well, then sweat in a little oil and butter and freeze. Good combined with shredded cabbage. Fantastic in soups. Lends sweetness to purées. A veg for the stockpot (see pages 236–8), too.	Pages 111, 134, 201, 208, 210
Lettuce	May–October	In the fridge for a day or two	Ubiquitous in salads, of course, but also amazingly tasty cooked: try in soups, risottos, pasta dishes, stir-fries – even purées.	Pages 109, 123, 161
Nettles Pick out the young nettle tips only	March–April	In a plastic bag in the fridge for 24 hours	Wearing rubber gloves, wash well, discarding stalks. Then cook as spinach (sting disappears on cooking).	Page 126
Parsnips	September–March	In a cool room for a week, in the fridge for up to 2 weeks	Delicious roasted – ideal in fat chunks for babies or as a purée (see page 106). Excellent made into soup. Slice paper-thin and bake to make crisps.	Pages 108, 177, 209
Peas 1kg pods yields about 400g peas	June–August	In the fridge for a day or two, but they lose sweetness all the while	Lovely raw on their own or in salads (can be a choking risk for babies). Make into soup or purée (see page 106). Add to frittata, curries or risotto. Or blanch lightly and freeze. Use empty pea pods in stock.	Pages 108, 124, 161, 180, 204
Pears	August–January Conference dominate, but Williams, Concorde and Comice are lovely varieties to look out for	In the fruit bowl for up to a week, depending on how hard they are when you buy them (all pears are picked under-ripe). Check daily to catch the point of perfect tenderness	Steam and purée (see page 105). Bake, poach or roast for puddings. Can be added to pies and crumbles, along with apple, or combined with late raspberries and blueberries for a fruit salad. Good with roasted meat, too.	Pages 112, 172, 196

Food	In season	Storage	Got a glut?	Recipes
Peppers	August–November	In the fridge for a week or so	Good raw as a finger food. Or roast and skin, then purée or chop. Fantastic in soups or sauces, and great in salads with cheese.	Pages 153, 177, 186, 203
Plums and Greengages	July–September	In a cool room or the fridge for a day or two	Cook to an intense purée (see page 106). Eat plain or with yoghurt, custard, ice cream etc, or stir a little into stews, tagines or curries. Alternatively, halve the fruit and roast with a little butter and vanilla. Never give to small children without removing stone first.	Pages 142, 170, 192
Potatoes, new	May–July	Remove plastic packaging and put in a paper or cloth bag; keep in the dark, in a cool room, for up to a week	Great roasted, or cooked and crushed with butter or oil and garlic. Perfect for frittatas. Also good cooked and thinly sliced on pizza.	Pages 124, 164
Potatoes, main crop	Harvested August–October, available all year round	Remove plastic packaging and put in a paper or cloth bag; keep in the dark, in a cool room, for a week or two	Peeled and roasted, in large chunks or 'chips', good as a first finger food. Parboiled potatoes can be frozen, then defrosted and roasted.	Pages 182, 191, 201, 209, 219
Purple sprouting broccoli	March–May	In the fridge for 1–2 days	Trim well. Steam, purée (see page 105) and freeze in portions. Good with pasta and for dipping. Or cook, then top with a little cheese sauce (see page 207) and grill.	Pages 122, 123, 132, 161, 162, 204
Quince	September–November	In a cool room for a week or two, or in the fridge for several weeks	Peel, core and chop, then cook to a purée with a little water. Will need sweetening – try adding apple or plum purée, or a little sugar or honey.	
Radishes	April–September	In the fridge for a day or two	Only worth eating if really fresh, then delicious raw – whole, grated or finely sliced.	
Raspberries (tayberries, loganberries)	July–October	In the fridge for 2–3 days	Open-freeze, then pack in tubs. Add to crumbles, muffins and smoothies.	Pages 113, 144, 170, 192

Food	In season	Storage	Got a glut?	Recipes
Rhubarb	January–April (indoor, forced), April–September (outdoor)	In the fridge for several days	Freeze stems raw, or roast until soft, then purée. It will need sweetening – use apple or plum purée, or a little sugar or honey.	Pages 113, 142, 170
Salsify and Scorzonera	October–November	In a cool room or the fridge for a few days	Peel and roast. Or add to other roots in roasts, gratins or soups.	Page 106
Spinach	All year round, depending on variety	In the fridge for a couple of days	Wilt in minimum amount of boiling water, drain, squeeze out liquid and chop. Add to pasta, pies, curry, pizza and frittata.	Pages 109, 126, 151, 180, 210
Squashes and Pumpkins	September–February	In a cool place, for weeks	Roast in wedges for salads or as finger food (remove skin). Great cubed in risotto. Purée (see page 107). Or use for soups, or mash as alternative to spuds.	Pages 111, 176, 177, 182, 195, 204, 208
Strawberries	May–August	Lose flavour if refrigerated, so keep in a cool room for a day or two	These don't freeze well whole, so purée and use to make frozen yoghurt or combine with other fruit purées and serve with yoghurt.	Pages 113, 148, 192
Swede	October–February	In a cool room for a week or so, or the fridge for several weeks	Peel, boil and mash with butter and black pepper. Purée plain for babies. Add to veg soups and to other roots for roasting.	Page 106
Sweetcorn	August–September	In the fridge for a day or two, but loses sweetness all the while	Slice off kernels, blanch for 1 minute, open-freeze and pack in tubs. Good in soups. Or try creamed corn (see page 158).	Pages 158, 182
Tomatoes	June–October	Lose flavour if refrigerated, so keep in a cool room for a few days	Roast with garlic and herbs, then push through a sieve; use this intense tomato purée as a base for sauces or soups. Use cherry tomatoes as finger foods for toddlers.	Pages 162, 165, 177, 188, 191, 204, 212
Turnips	July–December	In the fridge for a week or so	Young turnips are good roasted or braised in stock, and can also be eaten raw, grated or finely sliced.	

Things to Avoid

I'm not suggesting that you should become a food detective, scanning each meal, snack and treat for potential health risks, but there are a few things that you might want to limit and a few you might want to avoid altogether.

E-numbers

E-numbers are food additives that have been approved for use by the EU. The E-number labelling system covers hundreds of substances. Some seem fairly benign: things like pectin (E440) extracted from fruit, or agar (E406) from seaweed, for example. Some Es are most useful: raising agents such as baking powder in particular. And some are even technically nutritious: vitamin C, or E300, is widely used as an antioxidant, for instance. But some are controversial: the safety of the sweetener aspartame (E951) has been seriously questioned and others have been strongly associated with health problems in children. It often seems to be combinations of additives, even ones that seem innocuous on their own, that have serious effects.

The work involved in assessing the potential outcome of every possible combination of E-numbers is, of course, almost beyond comprehension. So, either you need to become an expert on what all the hundreds of different E-numbers stand for, and what these ingredients might do, or you can simply try and avoid them as much as possible. After all, what we're talking about here is largely a collection of artificial colourings and flavourings, emulsifiers, stabilisers, gums, thickeners and sweeteners. Not a particularly enticing menu. And a pot of fruit purée with added E300 is hardly the same as a fresh apple, packed with its own natural vitamin C.

Even if you don't adopt a general avoidance policy, there are certain Es parents should be particularly aware of because they have been specifically linked to health problems in children. Research at Southampton University in 2007 suggested that consuming a combination of some of the following additives could lead to increased hyperactivity in some children: tartrazine (E102), ponceau 4R (E124), sunset yellow (E110), carmoisine (E122), allura red (E129), quinoline yellow (E104) and sodium benzoate (E211). These are all colourings, except for sodium benzoate, which is a preservative. In addition, there are some sweeteners which, if eaten to excess, can cause diarrhoea, especially in young children: sorbitol (E420), xylitol (E967), maltitol (E965), sucralose (E955) and isomalt (E953). At food.gov.uk you can access a list of all the E-numbers and the additives they relate to.

Sugar, salt and the wrong kind of fat

Too much salt is very bad for anyone, and particularly for babies, whose kidneys just can't cope with it. You'll find details of how much is enough on pages 68–9. Salt levels are limited in food specifically marketed for babies, but not in everyday, child-friendly staples such as bread, cheese, houmous and oatcakes, which all contain a significant amount. These foods don't need to be banned, just controlled. Items which tend to be really high in salt include ready-made sauces, ready meals, processed meats and crisps.

Too much sugar, particularly refined sugar, is not a good thing either (more of this on pages 70–2). Be aware that sugar goes under many names on an ingredients label: anything that ends in 'ose', such as sucrose, maltose or dextrose, is a sugar, as is corn syrup or any other kind of syrup, as well as fruit juice concentrate, honey, molasses and maltodextrin.

Babies and young children shouldn't follow a low-fat diet (see page 61), but they don't need too much saturated fat, or any hydrogenated fat at all. In moderate quantities, saturated animal fats from minimally processed sources, such as red meat, eggs, cream or butter, can be a useful source of calories and vitamins. The hydrogenated fats found in some processed foods are a different matter. Hydrogenation turns liquid vegetable oils into solid fats; the process also creates things called artificial trans fats which have been linked to an increased risk of heart disease.

Processed foods

The good news is that it's fairly easy to steer clear of all the undesirable extras mentioned above, if you avoid processed foods. Now, to be fair, 'processed' is a tricky description because a great deal of the food we eat has been processed in some way – including healthy ingredients like dried pulses, tinned tomatoes, organic cheese and yoghurt. When I talk about processed foods to avoid, I really mean convenience foods – those in which most of the preparation has already been done by the manufacturer – fruit-flavoured yoghurts, ready meals and pre-prepared sauces, crisps, chocolates, sweets, ready-made cakes and biscuits, fizzy drinks and fruit squashes. The breastfeeding organisation La Leche League sum it up best when they describe good nutrition as 'eating a well-balanced and varied diet of foods in as close to their natural state as possible'.

Don't start tearing your hair out if your child enjoys the odd plate of baked beans on toast. But I think it's wise to try to keep these foods as occasional items, and prioritise home-made food where you can.

The First Year

The great food adventure begins

WEANING, the gradual transition a baby makes from milk alone to solid foods, is an exciting time. Beginning to eat solid food is a developmental milestone, of course, but it also marks a deepening and enhancement of family relationships. As the youngest member starts to take an active part in shared meals, they find a new opportunity to express their personality, interacting more with everyone else. So weaning isn't just about food, it's about eating – in the broadest sense. Making mealtimes positive, enjoyable experiences is one of the most important things you can do in preparing your child for the life that lies ahead of them.

A positive weaning experience can begin before you've even thought about apple purée or carrot sticks. You can involve your baby in mealtimes just by having them with you when you eat. The way that you breast- or bottle-feed may also influence the way they explore solid food when the time comes. This chapter looks at weaning as a process, not an event, and demonstrates my belief that your baby should really lead the way.

Baby Milk

It's quite possible that you may be reading this book before you've even had your first baby, and you might still be making up your mind whether to breastfeed, formula-feed, or do a bit of both. Given that I am a passionate advocate of breastfeeding, I would do my best to nudge you in the direction of exclusive breastfeeding. But I know there are a host of reasons for choosing formula, and I would never judge any mother who does so. Breastfeeding may be a better choice, but it doesn't make you a better parent.

In all probability you will already have taken some decisions on the subject, though the choices you make about milk-feeding may not be limited to the first few months of your baby's life. Many parents start thinking about choosing a formula during the second half of their baby's first year, which is why I've included some information on it here.

Breastfeeding

Breastfeeding is, I think, the soundest possible foundation for good eating later in life, not least because it protects a child's health. It also aids the development of the facial and oral muscles and, because the flavour of breastmilk varies depending on what the mother eats, some experts believe breastfed babies are more ready to investigate a range of solid foods. One of the other great benefits of breastfeeding, if you do it on demand, is that it enables a baby to regulate their own feeding, to respond to their body's messages of hunger and fullness. Just as importantly, it encourages you, the parent, to trust your baby's signals too, which should lead to a more relaxed approach to weaning.

How long you breastfeed your child for is entirely up to you (and them). The benefits are on-going. While breastmilk is not enough on its own to sustain a one- or two-year-old, it remains an excellent source of nutrition, and the immune-boosting properties continue. So even if you supplement with formula milk, any breastmilk at all is good.

Don't feel that you're obliged to give up breastfeeding at 6 months if you don't want to, or because every other mother you know has done so. And don't feel that you can't ask for help and information about breastfeeding just because your baby has gone beyond the newborn stage. The breastfeeding support available in this country (and there is plenty of it, if you know where to look) is not just there for the first few weeks. At any time, if you encounter problems or difficulties, if you are wondering what is normal, what to expect or what to do next, there are many resources to help you (see page 249).

Expressing milk Once your baby is a few months old and breastfeeding is well established, you can express your milk using a pump. Store it carefully in the fridge or freezer and it can then be fed to your baby in a bottle or cup if you're not around. A lot of mums express milk for their baby when they return to work. I've got to be honest, expressing milk is one of the least fun things I've ever done, but some mums find it easy – and it's a good way to extend the benefits of breastfeeding. Expressed milk can also be a useful ingredient when you're first preparing solid food for your child.

Formula feeding

Until they are 12 months old, a baby who is not breastfed must be given formula milk. There is no other nutritionally adequate substitute for breastmilk. So if you decide to stop or cut back on breastfeeding at any point during the first year, you will need to choose a proprietary 'infant milk'. Most are based on cow's milk, modified to make it more like human milk, and fortified with essential nutrients, such as vitamins and iron.

There's a big range of different formulas on the shelves. Again, I could fill a whole chapter on the subject of what's in them, but the nuts and bolts of it are that most are essentially pretty similar. Although manufacturers will use all sorts of clever marketing tools to persuade you to buy their brand rather than someone else's, it's important to realise that a higher price or glossier packaging doesn't mean the formula is better quality or more nutritious. All UK infant milks are nutritionally complete and must adhere to the same rules on composition; i.e. they are all good enough.

If your baby is 6 months or older and you are considering choosing a formula, you are also likely to come across products labelled as 'follow-on' milk. These contain more iron and protein than standard formula. They are not suitable for babies under 6 months and they are not necessary even after that. A 'stage 1' infant formula is perfectly adequate up until the age of 12 months, or even beyond. The government's Scientific Advisory Committee on Nutrition (SACN) has stated that 'there is no scientific evidence demonstrating nutritional advantage' of follow-on milk over standard infant formulas. In part, this is because babies are not able to absorb all that extra iron.

So how do you choose? There are resources that will give you more information about exactly what goes into different brands of formula milk. I like infantfeeding.info, which includes useful tables listing ingredients in different formulas. A Royal College of Midwives booklet, Infant Feeding (available from rcm.org.uk), also includes a comparison table of some of the major brands.

Your choice of formula will probably be influenced most by the nature of the protein that's in it. There are two types of protein in cow's milk: whey protein and casein. These days, most formulas have more whey than casein. Whey is easier to digest than casein, as it forms softer curds in the baby's stomach. For this reason, most sources recommend using a whey-based formula. When it comes to selecting one brand of whey-based formula over another, you may well find that word-of-mouth advice from friends and fellow parents is as good a guide as any. Alternatively, you might simply want to choose the least expensive.

Casein-based milks are actually the older style of formula, common until whey-based ones were developed. They are marketed at 'hungry' babies, as 'second stage' milks, or as a means to 'delay early weaning'. They do not contain any more calories but, because they stay in the stomach for longer, they are supposed to be more satisfying. Casein-based formulas are usually given names such as 'Hungry', 'Second' or 'Plus'. However, as I've already said, a baby doesn't need to pass through 'stages' of formula.

You will also probably come across 'comfort' milks. These are partially hydrolysed; i.e. the protein has been broken down to some extent, to make it easier to digest. Marketed as being gentle on the tummy, they are aimed at unsettled, 'sicky', colicky or constipated babies. Whether they are effective or not is a matter of debate, and they are not suitable for a baby with a cow's milk protein allergy or intolerance. Lactose-free formulas are also available. These can still be based on cow's milk but with the milk sugar, lactose, replaced with another sugar. These may be prescribed if your baby proves to be lactose intolerant. In all cases, if you think your child is having trouble digesting formula, you should speak to your doctor.

'Growing-up' or 'toddler' milks are, like follow-on milks, fortified with extra iron and vitamins. 'Goodnight' formulas, which you may also find, are thickened with ingredients such as ground rice or potato starch. They are promoted as helping to 'settle' babies at bedtime. Again, there is no evidence that they offer a nutritional advantage over infant formulas, and the SACN has raised concerns that they 'encourage parents to believe that it is desirable for a baby to sleep longer at an age when healthy infants show considerable variation in normal sleeping behaviour'. They are not suitable for babies under 6 months.

Goat's milk preparations are not recommended for babies under 12 months, because they are not thought to be nutritionally adequate. Soya-based formulas should only be given on the advice of a health professional. They are generally given to babies who cannot have cow's milk protein and/or lactose, but many of those babies may react to soya too. There is also some concern about the presence of phytoestrogens in soya milk. These are naturally occurring substances which, some believe, may affect reproductive development if consumed in large amounts.

Feeding on demand

The advantages of demand-feeding are not confined to breastfed babies. While formula-fed babies are more likely to be fed on a schedule, and in regular, quantified amounts, they don't have to be. You can still apply the principles of demand feeding to a bottle-fed baby. Indeed that is what authorities such as the Royal College of Nursing suggest. Allowing your baby to feed according to their own appetite and to stop when they feel full lays the building blocks for a healthy and moderate style of eating later in life.

It's not so easy, of course, to demand-feed when you need to make up bottles first. Each bottle should be made up just before it's needed because storing made-up formula increases the risk of any bacteria present within it multiplying. Powdered infant formula is not sterile. It can contain harmful bacteria such as salmonella and E-coli. For this reason, it is essential to always mix it with water that's at least 70°C (i.e. boiled in a kettle then cooled for a few minutes) in order to kill bacteria. The milk will then need to be cooled before your baby can drink it.

If you have to make up a bottle in advance (and never do this for a very young or premature baby, who will be particularly vulnerable to infection), you must be scrupulous about hygiene, cool it quickly (hold the bottle, teat covered, under cold running water) and refrigerate the bottle below 5°C. Do not keep it for longer than 24 hours.

You must discard any formula left over from a feed within 2 hours. Don't reheat it. Ready-to-drink liquid formula, which is sterile, may be a better option if you're feeding on demand, but it is more expensive.

The importance of milk as your baby grows

Breast or formula milk should remain a very significant part of your child's diet for at least their first year. As you begin to wean your baby on to solid foods, continue to breast- or bottle-feed them as you have been – ideally on demand. In the early weeks or even months of weaning, they may not eat a great deal of solid food and will still need to get most of their nutrients and calories from milk. Solids should be a complement to it, not a replacement. Breast or formula milk can also be a useful ingredient in their first foods – ideal for mixing into a porridge or purée, for instance.

Current government advice is not to give ordinary cow's milk, straight from the bottle or carton, to babies under the age of 6 months. From then on, it's ok to use cow's milk in small quantities – in recipes, say – as long as your baby doesn't show signs of allergy or intolerance (see page 77). But cow's milk contains too much protein and salt, and not enough iron and vitamins, to be an alternative to breast or formula milk within the first 12 months. So only give it as a main drink after your baby reaches a year.

The First Solid Foods

With the benefit of hindsight, I wish I had worried less about what my babies were eating, and more about what mealtimes were actually like for them. It is important to offer your child a wide variety of healthy foods, and, as weaning progresses, to give them several opportunities to eat each day, but you don't have to get large amounts of food into them to start with – not for the first day, the first week, not even for the first few months, if you continue to milk-feed them on demand.

In fact, breast or formula milk can still provide up to half a baby's energy intake by the age of one, and can supply a significant part of their nutritional needs well into their second year. That doesn't mean you don't need to encourage them to eat a good range of nutritious solids – you do, because milk cannot supply all the nutrients they need after 6 months. But it does mean you don't need to panic if they don't seem to be consuming a great quantity at each meal.

Having said that, many babies take to food like ducks to water, in which case you just need to make sure they are still drinking plenty of milk too. A baby cannot physically take in enough solid food to meet all their nutritional needs at this stage.

When should you start weaning?

The short answer is: at around 6 months old. I think that's a sound guide and it's certainly what I went for. If, however, you want to know why we are advised to wean at 6 months – or you feel you might want to wean earlier or later, do read on...

The current advice from the Department of Health, to start weaning when your baby is about 6 months old, is based on guidance from the World Health Organisation. The WHO states that exclusive breastfeeding for the first 6 months of life is best for a baby's health and development. The organisation's view is that breastmilk is fully adequate for an infant's needs up until 6 months – at which point, babies start to require more

nutrients (iron, in particular) than milk alone can provide. The WHO also points out that exclusive breastfeeding for 6 months protects against disease. In WHO literature on the subject, numerous studies are cited from various countries, including two that show babies who were breastfed exclusively for 6 months suffered less diarrhoea and less respiratory illness than those exclusively breastfed for only 3 or 4 months, respectively. In short, the WHO's view – and our own government's – is that the protective effects of exclusive breastfeeding should be capitalised on until the baby actually needs other foods.

There is little evidence as to how things might differ for a partially or fully formula-fed baby, but the government's Scientific Advisory Committee on Nutrition (SACN) says that there are unlikely to be any risks associated with weaning a formula-fed baby at 6 months either.

By 6 months, a baby's digestive system and kidneys are mature enough for foods other than breast or formula milk and they should be able to cope with solid food in their mouths. Indeed, they may well be capable of feeding themselves.

Some sources also say that weaning before 6 months may increase a child's risk of allergy. In fact, there is a lot of debate about this and new research is constantly emerging. The evidence concerning precisely the best time to wean, from an allergy-preventing point of view, is not clear, though experts agree that weaning should not begin before 4 months. For now, the government continues to advise waiting until around 6 months. It also makes clear that the foods most likely to cause allergy (listed on page 54) should not be given before 6 months because, in the experts' view, there is no evidence that it is safe to do so.

While a lot of informed opinion states that it's a good idea to wait until 6 months, it's worth knowing that there are others who feel that this is the latest that weaning should begin. Some specialists believe it's a good idea to expose babies to new tastes before this age.

Dr Gillian Harris, Consultant Paediatric Clinical Psychologist at the Children's Hospital, Birmingham, feels strongly that starting solids at 6 months is cutting things a bit fine. She says: 'I believe that introducing solids between 4 and 6 months is important. There is no evidence that it increases the risk of allergies. Babies are least neophobic (afraid of new foods) at this age. The evidence shows that giving lots of different tastes very early on – and just a taste is fine – increases the child's readiness to accept a range of foods later.'

I think parents should also know about a 2007 study by The European Society of Paediatric Gastroenterology, Hepatology and Nutrition (ESPGHAN). This well-respected scientific body reviewed the evidence that related to healthy children in specifically European populations. Their conclusions supported the idea that 'exclusive or full breastfeeding for about 6 months is a desirable goal'. However, they also stated that 'complementary feeding (solids) should not be introduced before 17 weeks or later than 26 weeks', for nutritional and developmental reasons.

I'm not suggesting for a minute that you should introduce solids before 6 months if you don't think your baby is ready, but if you feel they may be inclined sooner, you don't have to feel like a pariah. Talk to your doctor or health visitor first, and you may feel happy about weaning a bit earlier.

One of the most important things, when you are making up your mind about the best time to wean, is to observe your baby carefully. They will give out signs of readiness, including the ability to sit up straight (alone or with some support), and to hold their head up, chewing on their fists or on toys. You may notice the loss of the 'tongue-thrust reflex', whereby anything put into the baby's mouth is automatically pushed out again, and an interest in trying food when it's made available to them.

Many people cite a baby waking in the night having previously slept through, or demanding a lot more milk than they have been, as signs of 'hunger' for solids. But you have to be careful here. If a five-month old baby really is hungry, it's best to give them more milk before you start thinking about pear purée. Milk is much richer in calories and nutrients than the kind of solid foods they're likely to be eating at first and experts agree that the first stages of weaning are about exposure to new tastes, and getting used to the idea of food, rather than racking up the calories. Night-waking and other signs of dissatisfaction can be caused by teething, illness, a growth spurt, or your baby simply feeling a bit unsettled. Don't automatically assume they signal a readiness for solids.

To sum up the advice on when to start weaning:

- Do not wean before 4 months (17 weeks). A baby's system is simply not ready at this stage and weaning could increase the risk of allergies and illness, not to mention choking.

- It's probably best not to begin weaning later than 6 months (26 weeks). Watch your baby and be guided by your own feelings about whether or not they're ready.

- Bear in mind your baby's gestational age at birth: a baby born at 38 weeks is considered full-term, as is one born at 42 weeks, but the latter has actually had a month more growing time.

- If your baby was born prematurely always seek advice from your doctor about the best time to wean – their needs may be quite different to a term baby.

- If you want to begin weaning between 4 and 6 months, talk to your health visitor or doctor first. The government still advises against giving babies certain foods before 6 months – the ones most commonly linked to allergies.

- Whenever you start, go slowly and gradually. Introduce new foods in small quantities, one at a time to start with, so you can see if your baby has an adverse reaction to any of them.

- If your baby seems really unreceptive or unhappy with solid food, leave it a few days and try again. This should be a fun, positive experience for everyone!

'Nell was always nosy about food. She would sit at the table with us and we'd feed her puréed veg, but she'd often have a tiny bit of whatever we were eating too. We didn't push her to eat anything, and some days she ate more than others, but she would always play and experiment. We didn't worry about quantities because the solids were on top of breastfeeding, not instead of it.'
Mark, dad to Nell, 3

'Lex didn't really eat much until he was about 14 months old. It was stressful at times, but he was growing, so I knew it didn't really matter. Then suddenly it was like a switch was flicked and he went from having mainly milk to mainly food, almost overnight.'
Mac, mum to Lex, 3, and Tilly, 1

'Alexander was a gobbler right from the start. He showed no interest in food until he was almost 6 months, then suddenly started taking three hearty meals a day – spreading them all over himself and the table.'
Rachel, mum to Alexander, 2, and Catherine, 5 months

How should you go about weaning?

There are two main schools of thought on weaning. The conventional way is to start off feeding babies wet purées on a spoon and encourage them to gradually accept lumpier textures before trying 'normal' foods that the rest of the family is eating. However, there is a very different approach known as baby-led weaning, which you could call 'new', though some would argue is actually far older than the conventional method.

Baby-led weaning eschews the spoon-feeding of purées altogether and instead recommends simply offering a baby the same kind of food the rest of the family is eating, and letting them feed themselves. So, rather than spooning parsnip purée into their mouth, you'd lie a few fingers of tender, roasted parsnip in front of them and let them make their own explorations.

In arguments about weaning, the focus on the texture of the food – whether it's puréed or not – is slightly misleading. After all, we all eat purées: pâtés, dips, spreads, soups – these are normal family fare. It's not really purées themselves that baby-led weaning defines itself against, it is the spoon-feeding of them. That emphasis on giving the baby control over what and how much they eat is what I really value about baby-led weaning, and it is something that can be applied no matter what you choose to feed them.

Foods such as porridge, yoghurt or puréed fruit and veg can be put on a spoon (or a breadstick, or your finger) and offered for a baby to feed themselves – something they may be able to do from quite early on. In short, although baby-led weaning focuses on grabbable finger foods, I think it is perfectly possible to be 'baby-led' and still own a blender.

For what it's worth, I was a keen and slightly dogmatic baby-led weaner myself and rather anti-purée. With the experience of two children under my belt, I know that if I ever had another, I'd be much more ready to try mashed and puréed foods early on, as well as finger foods.

Traditional spoon-feeding

If you wean much before 6 months, you'll probably have to at least begin with spoon-feeding as your baby is unlikely to be able to feed themselves or to cope with anything other than soft purées. Whatever age you start, this method also gives you, the parent, much more control over what your child is eating. You can purée almost any ingredients you fancy. It allows you to get lots of different tastes into your baby's mouth, or at least onto their lips – because you'll be putting them there.

With spoon-feeding your child is likely to eat more, in the early stages at least, than if you just let them feed themselves. That's not necessarily a good thing, though, as their solid food will probably be less nutrient-dense than the milk you're giving them. In addition, it's possible to spoon more food into your baby than they really want or need.

Baby-led weaning

This is the ultimate way to allow a baby to begin eating at their own pace and to eat only what they need. It should make weaning fun and relaxed and thereby foster a happy and positive relationship with food.

Here are some points to consider:

- Wait until 6 months, or certainly close to it. Your baby needs to be able to sit up straight and hold their head up.

- Some babies really don't like being spoon-fed, and will refuse food offered in this way. In certain cases, letting them feed themselves is the only way forward.

- Eating finger foods and lumpy, textured things is good for a child's development as they learn how to pick up food, get it into their mouth and chew it.

- This approach requires you to put your trust in your child. You have to let them lead the way, which can be scary – particularly when it seems as though they're not eating much at all. But if you continue to breastfeed or bottle-feed whenever they want it, you'll be providing good nutritional back-up.

It's an undeniable fact that some parents feel anxious about letting a baby eat non-puréed food because of the fear of choking. It's a valid fear and I think if it really stresses you out, then baby-led weaning is not for you. There simply isn't any research to show whether choking is more or less likely with different methods of weaning. Small babies can only suck. They then gradually develop the ability to chew and to control food in their mouths, so by 6 months they should be ready to tackle their first finger foods. This is another reason why baby-led weaning is definitely recommended as a six-months-plus approach. And, of course, you have to choose foods that are appropriate: soft, steamed vegetables, or tender fruits to start with, for example.

Like many other baby-led weaners, I believe that allowing a baby to control what goes into their own mouth can actually make choking less likely. If they have the motor skills to pick something up, then they should have the oral skills to chew it. The 'pincer grip', for instance, that allows them to pick up small things such as peas and sultanas, is very unlikely to be present in a six-month old.

Whatever your approach, you do have to introduce your child to chunky food at some point. There are lots of ways to minimise the risk of choking – the most important being that you should NEVER leave them alone while eating – and these are relevant to all babies, however they're weaned. See page 56 for more detail on this.

If you want to know more about traditional weaning, talking to those who have already done it is probably the best way. Standard texts, such as the Department of Health's *Birth to Five* booklet, and the government's weaning web pages (eatwell.gov.uk/agesandstages/baby/weaning), also focus on this approach. If you want to know more about baby-led weaning, then Gill Rapley's book *Baby-Led Weaning* is an ideal resource. In addition, you will find unlimited information and discussion about it on the internet, including lots of video clips which will give you a good idea of what to expect.

However, I believe that the more you look into it, the more you'll find something of an overlap between the two approaches. My researches suggest that many people actually employ a combination of conventional and baby-led weaning techniques. The parents who seem happiest about their own weaning choices are the ones who have responded to their baby's individual needs and capabilities, and who have the confidence to say, 'this is what works for us'.

In any case, the spoon-feeding question is really only an issue during the first stage of weaning. All weaning strategies have the same aim: to get your child to eat a healthy, balanced, grown-up range of foods. Pretty much all sources, no matter what their stand on spoons, agree that introducing texture, giving thick or lumpy food and encouraging your baby to feed themselves with finger foods, should be done early; i.e. from 6 or 7 months. It's widely accepted that babies are much more accepting of new tastes and textures in the early days and they tend to 'close down' on new things at around 9–10 months. There's evidence that babies who don't encounter lumpy foods or finger foods by the age of 9 months are more likely to be 'fussy' eaters later on.

However you go about weaning, the following core principles apply:

- Observe your child's signals when deciding if it's time to introduce solids.

- Don't ever force food into your child's mouth.

- Give your child every opportunity to explore their food with their hands and feed themselves as soon as they want to.

- Expose your child to a wide variety of tastes, from as early as possible.

- Start to include finger foods, textured foods and lumpy foods from about 6 months.

- Where possible, give your child the same food you are eating (puréed or not), and share the meal with them.

'I spoon-fed my first daughter until she was about 9 months old. With my second, I started doing the same thing, but I began to question it. I thought, "here we go again, months and months of purées". I looked up baby-led weaning and thought I'd try it. I held off until she was about 5½ months and she could sit up and she'd started to take food off me. She was ready, and that was it. Jasmin really enjoys eating now. I'm so proud of her, and it's a real pleasure not to have to sit there spoon-feeding.'
Becky, mum to Isabel, 3 and Jasmin, 7 months

'The idea of baby-led weaning can be a bit ideological. Tell people you're doing it and they say, "Oh, you're that kind of parent", but lots of people are doing it – it's just finger foods! For us, it was a great way to introduce food as Martha absolutely would not take a spoon. I tried offering a piece of avocado, then broccoli, then carrot, and she went for it.'
Harriet, mum to Joe, 2 and Martha, 8 months

'We started weaning when Beth was 5 months old. We did purées. I'd heard lots of chat about finger foods but when we did try them, she would just cram things in to her mouth and gag on them. There were a couple of scary moments when I thought she was choking. I think she's just that kind of eater – even now, I have to remind her to chew things!'
Katie, mum to Beth, 3

The very first foods

Most babies' first foods are very simple meals of fruits or vegetables. These are gentle on the tummy and easy to prepare. They also encompass a range of different tastes – including bitter and sour notes – all important for your baby to experience. Popular ones are listed below, but you could try others. Avoid berries, tomatoes, citrus fruits, pineapple and kiwi to start with (see page 76).

Try beginning with a once-a-day piece or purée of a single type, or try offering both a solid piece and a purée together. If you're puréeing, keep the texture pretty loose and liquid to start with, thinning down with breast or formula milk if necessary, then increase the thickness and texture as your baby gets to grips with eating. You'll find guidelines for cooking and puréeing various fruit and veg on pages 101–7.

Try the following:

- Steamed broccoli, puréed, or as whole florets

- Steamed cauliflower, puréed, or as whole florets

- Well-cooked whole green beans

- Steamed and puréed apple

- Ripe, soft pear, peeled and cored – raw, in whole slices, or steamed then puréed

- Boiled, baked or roasted potato or sweet potato – skin removed, in wedges or batons, or mashed

- Banana, cut into chunks or sticks, or mashed

- Cucumber sticks, skin removed

- Steamed, boiled or roasted carrot or parsnip, or baked beetroot (a particularly messy one!), in sticks or puréed

- Not-too-ripe avocado in wedges, or ripe avocado – mashed

- Plum, peach, apricot or nectarine, halved or quartered and stone removed, or cooked and puréed

- Cooked and puréed peas

- Cooked and puréed lentils or split peas

Choose a time when your baby is not tired, grumpy or hungry; give a milk feed a little while beforehand, so they are alert and comfortable and ready to explore. Have them sitting upright. Offer them some food, don't force it upon them: put finger foods in front of them, put soft foods on a spoon and gently touch it to their lips or let them pick it up. Be attentive and responsive to your baby's reaction (never leave them alone with food) and let them take the lead.

What happens next?

What should you expect from the day when you first offer your baby some solid food? Some children launch into eating pretty much straight away, some are wary, some want nothing to do with it. Don't worry, and don't force the issue. Remember that eating is a totally new experience to them – they don't even know what food is. As far as they're concerned, it's an interesting new substance to be explored and played with. They have no idea that swallowing it will stop them being hungry. In fact, in the early days, you shouldn't try offering them solid foods when they are obviously hungry or they may find it difficult to focus on this new challenge.

Initially, you'll probably find that at least 90 per cent of what goes into your baby's mouth comes straight out again. They may be more interested in touching the food with their hands than putting it in their mouths. They may get bored or tired quickly. Sometimes, they won't be up for eating at all. These things will gradually change as they grow and develop and start to learn what eating is all about. Go at your baby's pace and keep reminding yourself that solids do not need to form a large part of their nutritional intake to start with – that's what the milk-feeding is for. Be encouraging, but don't feel you need to squeal with delight and give a standing ovation every time they swallow – keep mealtimes relaxed and try not to let the mess bother you.

Different babies take different amounts of solid food, just as they take different amounts of milk. Don't get hung up on quantities. For the first few meals, they might not eat anything. Certainly, don't expect them to take more than a teaspoon or two of something soft, or to gnaw on something solid. As you go on and start to observe your baby's eating habits, you'll get a good idea of the quantity that's right for them. Let them eat until they want to stop, and don't cajole them to eat more than they want. Try to relax and let them get on with it. Babies know how to regulate their own intake and, if you don't interfere, should be able to keep doing so.

How to progress

Once your baby is happy with the idea of eating some solids, gradually start to offer food a little more often, and increase the range of tastes and textures. It's also important to try to get plenty of iron-rich foods (see page 62) into their meals from 6 months onwards, as the reserves they were born with will be running low.

Try the following:

- Any of the mixed fruit and veg purées on pages 107–13

- Toast, perhaps with a dip or spread based on meat or pulses

- Breadsticks (see pages 229–31)

- Purées of cooked pulses and vegetables

- Cooked or raw fruit puréed with plain yoghurt or freshly cooked rice

- Bone-free chicken, beef, pork, lamb, venison or fish – finely chopped or mashed, or in large strips or chunks to be held and gnawed or sucked

- Well-cooked eggs: mashed or sliced hard-boiled egg, or omelette strips

- Sticks of cheese (avoid very salty ones)

- Well-cooked noodles or pasta – plain or with a little meat or veg sauce

- Tofu, mashed or in large chunks

You'll find more info on the few foods to avoid, and why, on pages 74–5. But the basics are: don't give them honey, don't add any salt to their food, don't give whole or chopped nuts and make sure any eggs, fish or meat are thoroughly cooked.

If your baby is amenable, you can increase the complexity of their diet quite quickly. There are some foods, listed overleaf, that you might choose to introduce carefully, one by one, and a few that carry a choking risk (see page 56), but there's still very little that's off the menu. Before long, you can start to offer your little one much the same things the rest of the family is eating. You can start using recipes – or cooking 'proper' meals, if you like – as soon as you feel your baby is ready to begin experimenting beyond those first simple flavours and textures – probably at around 7 months, but it depends on them. You can adapt family food for babies where

necessary: this is often simply a case of chopping or mashing things up –
or, conversely, offering food in large chunks that your baby can grab and
chew. Some recipes are unsuitable for very young babies but, in general,
I think it's best to decide what you want to cook, then work out how to
make it appropriate for your baby, rather than pick a 'baby-food' recipe
and then have to start worrying about what everyone else is going to eat.

Allergenic foods

Foods that are most liable to cause an allergic reaction should be carefully
introduced – in a small amount, on their own, or alongside foods that you
know your child can eat happily, so you can note and take heed of any
reaction. But current government advice is that you can start introducing
them from 6 months in a suitable form (see foods to avoid giving, page
75), even if you have a history of allergies in your family.

The following foods are the ones most often linked to allergies:

- Peanuts (if your child has already been diagnosed with another allergy,
  such as eczema, or there are allergies in your family, the government
  still advises that you talk to your doctor before introducing peanuts)

- Tree nuts (brazils, hazelnuts, walnuts etc)

- Seeds

- Eggs

- Cow's milk

- Soya

- Wheat and other gluten-containing cereals such as oats, rye and barley

- Fish and shellfish

- It's also possible to be allergic to celery, lupin and mustard seed (very
  rare in the UK), and to kiwi fruit (again, rare here, but on the increase)

Ages and stages

Weaning is sometimes viewed as a process of distinct stages, but I think
it is impossible to say what your baby should be eating at any particular
point in time. Babies are individuals and develop at their own pace, but
if you are looking for some idea of what to expect, here's a rough guide:

AGE	FOOD
17–24 weeks (4–6 months)	Many parents wouldn't choose to wean their baby this young. But, if you do, they should probably be eating smooth purées.
24–26 weeks (6 months)	If your baby has been eating smooth purées, this is the time to try thickening them up and adding more texture. If you're starting spoon-feeding now, begin with smooth purées, but thicken them up fairly soon. If you want to try the baby-led weaning approach, this is the time to think about starting.
26–30 weeks (6–7 months)	Start offering your baby some finger foods around now – either as a complement to spoon-feeding, or on their own (baby-led weaning).
36 weeks (9 months)	By this point, it's important that your baby has experienced at least some textured, lumpy food and some finger food. Ideally, their diet should not be based on purées by now, and they should be eating textured foods such as thick porridge, mashed potato, risottos, fishcakes, bolognese and rice pudding. Encourage them to use a spoon themselves, and offer finger foods like bread, well-cooked pasta, pears, avocado, cheese, felafel or roasted vegetables.

What about milk?

However you wean, you should also continue to breast- or formula-feed your child as you have been. As they begin to take more solids, they will need less milk. But any reduction you make should be in response to them and should be done gradually. Do not drastically reduce milk feeds in an attempt to get them to eat more solids. Milk-feeding them whenever they want ensures they're not going short and means you can allow them to explore food at their own pace. You may want to give them a vitamin supplement too (see page 63).

By the end of their first year, children should still be taking plenty of milk – aim for at least 500ml formula for bottle-fed babies. It's impossible to tell how much milk breastfed babies are getting, of course, so simply continue to feed on demand.

Choking

Most parents, when they start offering their child solid food, will at some point experience anxiety over choking. It's a justifiable fear. Choking does happen: in the UK, somewhere in the region of 7,500 children under five visit hospital due to food-choking incidents each year. Most of these cases are fairly minor, but a tiny proportion prove fatal. That doesn't mean you should keep your child on a liquid diet – babies have to get used to eating.

Steps you can take to help prevent choking:

- Regardless of what they're eating, your baby should always be sitting upright when they have food, and you should always stay with them while they eat. Parental supervision is the best safety measure. Avoid feeding small children when they are overexcited or distressed. Don't let them eat while they're crawling, walking or running around, or watching television.

- Don't force food into their mouths.

- Babies can easily gag on food – some babies gag a lot – but that is not the same thing as choking, which occurs when a piece of food actually blocks the windpipe. It can be very scary to see your child gag or retch and cough up food, but it's part of the process of learning how to eat. Gagging is not dangerous: it's your baby's way of not choking.

- The greatest cause of choking in children is sweets – so that's one good reason to avoid them.

- Whole or chopped nuts are another real choking risk and should be off the menu before about 5 years of age.

- Beyond that, there are various foods that could, potentially, cause choking. (Though of course any food could, potentially, be a culprit.) While your baby's chewing skills are still developing, avoid anything that worries you. Foods most likely to cause choking are small, firm and round: whole grapes and blueberries, chickpeas, small cherry tomatoes, peas, popcorn, olives, raisins and sultanas. Chunks of raw apple, celery or carrot may also cause a problem – cut these into thin sticks, or grate them instead. Bones should be carefully removed from fish and meats such as chicken or rabbit, and sausages, burgers or tough meat can also be hard to chew and swallow.

- Use your instincts to judge what you should offer your child and when. You will be able to observe your baby's developing eating skills. All children are different – my elder daughter was a very competent chewer from an early age, while my younger still gagged on things fairly regularly at 2 years old.

- Try not to let a fear of choking limit your child's diet too much. Arm yourself with up-to-date knowledge of what to do if a baby does choke: www.redcross.org.uk and www.babycentre.co.uk are good reference sources. And keep a close eye on your child. As Nigella Lawson says in her chapter on feeding babies in *How to Eat*: 'vigilance is a better route than dietary censorship'.

Reluctant eaters

At what point should you start to worry about a baby's lack of interest in solid food? Probably not during the first year, unless they refuse solids altogether. It's true that neither breast nor formula milk provide all the calories and nutrients a baby needs beyond 6 months – particularly iron and vitamin D. But, if they're eating at least some solids each day, and you continue to breastfeed on demand or give at least 500ml formula a day, they shouldn't be going short.

Keep offering lots of different flavours and textures – even in very small amounts, these are important in building up acceptance of a range of foods. Make sure the foods you do serve are nutrient- and calorie-rich – try adding olive, rapeseed or walnut oil to purées, soups or dips, use plenty of full-fat dairy products and try to find a way to get meat or pulses into their diet. A vitamin supplement is recommended for all babies over 6 months anyway (see page 63), and if you give one it will help to take up the slack. You can also investigate fortified cereals if you're concerned about nutrient intake.

Persevere in offering your little one a variety of nutritious fare, keep mealtimes as pleasant as you can, and trust them to come round to solid foods when they're ready. If your child is lethargic, losing weight, not growing, dehydrated or showing signs of ill-health, if they seem to be showing real anxieties over food, or if you're at all worried about their development, then of course you should get them to a doctor quick-sharp. But if they're growing and developing normally, they're getting the right stuff from somewhere.

Nutrition

What exactly do young children need?

GOOD NUTRITION for children isn't vastly different from good nutrition for adults. There are a few things they need more of, and a few things they need less of, but it's not complicated. Providing a properly balanced, nutritious diet is pretty straightforward if you stick to the basic principles of variety and wholeness; i.e. lots of different foods in as fresh and unprocessed a state as possible.

The Five Food Groups

In general, we need a selection of foods from these five groups every day:

- Group 1: Starchy foods, such as bread, pasta, rice, potatoes
- Group 2: Fruit and vegetables
- Group 3: Protein, such as meat, fish, eggs, pulses, soya products
- Group 4: Dairy products
- Group 5: Fats and oils

Adults need a lot of groups 1 and 2, a reasonable amount of groups 3 and 4 and just a little of group 5. For babies and small children, the balance is slightly different.

Starchy foods

Under-fives are little power-houses of development and growth. They need lots of energy, so starchy, calorie-dense foods are important – plenty of bread, pasta, rice and cereals. For adults, consuming starches in a high-fibre, wholegrain form is highly recommended. For little children, that's not the case. Too much fibre can be over-filling and stop them eating other, nutrient-rich foods. Very high-fibre foods, such as bran cereals, can be hard for them to digest and may stop them absorbing nutrients. You don't have to ban all wholegrain foods, but try to combine white and wholemeal bread, pasta and rice, gradually shifting more to wholegrain foods as your child matures. Try my 25 per cent wholemeal bread (on page 229).

Fruit and veg

Offer lots of these, as they're packed with the vitamins your child needs to develop well. Brightly coloured types tend to contain more antioxidants and the World Health Organisation recommends including at least one dark green vegetable (spinach, broccoli, greens etc) or orange vegetable or fruit (carrot, pumpkin, pepper etc) every day, as these are rich sources of vitamin C, and of carotene, from which vitamin A is made. From around 12–18 months, the advice is for children to eat five portions a day of fruit and veg, just like adults – but child-sized portions. As a guide, a child's portion of fruit or veg will be roughly equivalent to the size of their palm.

Protein

Protein is what your body needs to quite literally build itself, so it's hugely important for a growing child. However, it's not needed in large quantities; if you make sure there's some protein in most meals, you should easily meet your child's requirements. If your child is vegetarian (by your design, or theirs) you do need to give protein a bit more thought. Meat and fish, as well as eggs and dairy, are rich in protein, and provide it in a 'complete' form; i.e. with all the amino acids the body needs. Other protein-rich foods such as pulses, nuts, seeds and grains provide 'incomplete' protein. It is still valuable, it's just that these protein foods need to be eaten in combination to make them 'complete'. One exception is the grain quinoa (pronounced 'keen-wa'). This is generally considered a complete source of protein, and highly nutritious in other ways too. Soy products, like tofu, are sometimes described as complete, but because their amino acid profile is not the same as an animal protein, combining soy with other protein foods is usually recommended. More on all this later, when I talk about vegetarian diets.

Dairy products

Dairy products provide calcium, protein, energy and B vitamins. You can start to introduce them gradually into your baby's diet from 6 months (see page 94 for advice on types of cheese). Assuming your child doesn't show any signs of dairy allergy or intolerance, the current advice is for small children to eat full-fat dairy products daily (in addition to breast or formula milk for the first year at least).

Fats and oils

A small child must not follow a low-fat diet. Around 40 per cent of their energy intake should come from fats and oils. Not only do these contribute the calories a child needs, they are also crucial for cell development, and provide fat-soluble vitamins and essential fatty acids. Don't be afraid to include a variety of fat sources in your child's diet, such as full-fat milk and dairy products, meat, oily fish, plant oils, nuts, seeds and avocados. Moderate amounts of saturated fats are fine for little ones, but it's better if they come from 'natural' sources, such as meat and dairy products, rather than from highly processed foods like commercially baked goods, biscuits and crisps. Include plenty of other, non-animal fats in your cooking too.

Do not give children reduced-fat yoghurt or milk, or any other low-fat products until they're at least 2 years old. You can then start to gradually reduce the amount of fat they have, and it's considered ok for them to eat a fairly low-fat diet from the age of about five onwards.

Omega fats and oily fish Omega-3 and omega-6 essential fatty acids are vital for all sorts of processes in the body. We get omega-3s from fish and seafood – oily fish is the richest source – as well as meat, dairy and eggs from free-ranging, grass-fed animals (grain-fed livestock tend to produce food containing less omega-3). Walnuts, walnut oil and flax oil are other sources. Dark green leafy veg also contain some omega-3, though in a form that's less easily absorbed by the body. We get omega-6 from meat, dairy products and eggs, as well as vegetable oils, nuts, seeds and grains.

Currently, most of us seem to get plenty of omega-6, but many people in this country lack omega-3 in their diet. That's why eating more fish, particularly oily fish like mackerel, sardines, herring, salmon and trout, is recommended. Oily fish is also a source of vitamins A and D, and iron – all nutrients which are sometimes lacking in children's diets. The latest advice is that we should all be eating oily fish every week, but not too much, as some oily fish may contain chemicals such as dioxins and PCBs, which accumulate over time in the body and could have adverse affects if consumed over long periods and at high levels. However, the known benefits of eating oily fish are considered to far outweigh the possible risks. You will find several recipes in this book which use mackerel – it's inexpensive, easy to cook and easy to de-bone. I've used salmon in a number of recipes too – it's simple to cook and extremely nutritious, but please see page 23 for a note on sustainability. Trout is a lovely fish but I hesitate to give it to small children because it's quite hard to rid it of all the bones prior to serving. The same is true of herring and fresh sardines.

Smoked fish, delicious though it may be, is high in salt, so I wouldn't give it to a baby, and I would use it judiciously with an older child.

Vitamins and Minerals

The best way to ensure your child is getting all the vitamins and minerals (or 'micronutrients') they need is simply to give them a varied diet based around the principles outlined above. But it's worth knowing about a few things in detail:

Iron is an essential nutrient and the one most likely to be lacking in a small child's diet. There is iron in breastmilk, and it's easily absorbed, but it's still not enough for a child over 6 months. Formula, likewise, does not provide sufficient iron after 6 months. Meat, poultry and oily fish are the richest and most easily-absorbed sources of iron. Pulses, green leafy veg, dried fruit and eggs provide iron but in a less easily absorbed form than meat. These foods should be paired with vitamin-C rich foods (fruits and vegetables), which aid the absorption of iron (see pages 67–8 for more on vegetarian diets).

Vitamin A is crucial for many functions, including vision, and there are concerns that some UK children are not getting enough. Offal and oily fish are good sources, but children should not eat these in large amounts. Orange and green fruits and vegetables contain carotene, which the body converts to vitamin A, so try to offer some of these every day.

Vitamin D is essential for healthy bones and teeth, and other functions. Eggs, offal and oily fish are among the few food sources – but these last two, again, should be eaten within limits. Our principal source is the sun – our bodies make this vitamin when the skin is exposed to sunlight – so there's a strong argument for careful, controlled exposure to sunshine to help children build up their vitamin D reserves.

Vitamin C is a powerful antioxidant. It also helps the body absorb iron from food. Vitamin C is abundant in all kinds of fresh fruit and veg, but levels in food can reduce drastically with age, so freshly harvested, local produce is an optimum source. Like many other vitamins, vitamin C is also affected by cooking, and contact with water or air, so give children raw fruit and veg where appropriate. However, cooked fruit and veg are still worthwhile sources. For ways to preserve maximum quantities of vitamins in food, see page 24.

Supplements

The Department of Health currently advises giving breastfed babies a supplement containing vitamins A, C and D, once they reach 6 months, and until they are about 5 years old. For formula-fed babies, supplements are recommended only once they are having less than 500ml formula a day, as formula is already fortified. The idea is that a supplement forms a safety net, supporting your child's developing system during the early stages of eating, when milk no longer offers complete nutrition and solid intake can be variable.

If your child is eating a really good range of fruit and veg (including lots of green and orange veg, see above), you could argue that they don't need a supplement of vitamins A and C. However, the case for giving vitamin D is more compelling, as it's not abundant in many foods. Our principal source is the sun, but many babies are extremely well-protected from this! If your child eats lots of vitamin D-rich foods such as oily fish and eggs, and gets plenty of sunshine, a vitamin D supplement may not be necessary. Others may benefit from one.

You can look at your local pharmacy for drops containing vitamins A, C and D which are suitable for babies from 6 months. However, it can be difficult to find them. A better option is probably to ask your health visitor about the NHS's inexpensive Healthy Start vitamin drops, which they should be able to get for you.

Some parents choose to give their children an iron supplement, but this nutrient is much better absorbed from food. Iron supplements can sometimes cause constipation or nausea and too much unabsorbed iron in the system can affect the balance of bacteria in the gut. If you're really concerned that your child may be deficient in iron, ask your doctor to do a blood test. If they prove to be anaemic, a supplement may be advised. Otherwise, focus on providing lots of iron-rich foods (see page 62).

Drinks

Until they are about 6 months old, your baby needs only breast or formula milk. Once they start taking solids, you should offer them drinks from a cup too, and all the current advice says these drinks should really be water – or full-fat milk for a child of 12 months-plus. (Be aware that some bottled mineral waters contain too much sodium for babies.)

Fruit juices are a less good option, and they are certainly not the same as eating fresh fruit. Even pure, fresh-pressed juices provide fruit sugar and fruit acid without fruit fibre. They are not brilliant for the teeth, especially if drunk between meals. Some children have a tendency to drink buckets of juice, if allowed, which means they then eat less. Excessive consumption of juice is also associated with diarrhoea and wind. If you do give juice, choose a pure one with no added sugar – or make your own at home with a juicer. Be wary of manufactured fruit drinks of the type specifically aimed at children – they can contain an awful lot of sugar, a number of preservatives and artificial sweeteners, and very little actual fruit juice.

Any juice that you give should be heavily diluted – one part juice to 10 parts water for babies. You can gradually reduce the water content as your child matures. Give juice in a cup, not a bottle, to minimise the amount of time the juice is in contact with your child's teeth. Try to keep it to mealtimes, when food and saliva will mitigate its effects, rather than for general slurping throughout the day.

Avoid fizzy drinks such as colas – they have no nutritional value and are full of sugar and additives. Even 'diet' brands still contain acids which attack teeth. Avoid tea and coffee, especially with meals, as they affect the absorption of iron – and no small child needs a caffeine buzz!

Continue to breastfeed your child for as long as you want to. If you're giving formula or stopping breastfeeding, you can switch to full-fat cow's milk as a main drink from 12 months.

Providing a Varied Diet

You're doing your job well if you provide a balanced diet, but that doesn't mean your child will eat it. Many children have very idiosyncratic eating patterns, and strong likes and dislikes. It's quite normal for even 'good' eaters to have mini food fads, eating nothing but fruit one day, then only toast and yoghurt the next. Little ones can view new things with suspicion, especially an unfamiliar dish. As I explain in the next chapter, strange foods can be quite frightening to them. Do not stress yourself over exactly what is eaten at each meal. If you want to get an idea of nutritional intake, take an overview and tot up what your child eats over the week.

The most important, number-one thing is to keep trying. Offer foods over and over again – in a no-fuss, neutral sort of way. Even if they've shoved spinach or tomatoes or chicken on the floor the last ten times you've offered them, keep going: calmly offering them, and sharing them, sending the message that these are things which are good to eat, and not in any way frightening. Babies have a natural preference for sweet tastes. Bitter and sour tastes need to be experienced many times before they become acceptable. But, for most children, most of the time, with most foods, acceptance will eventually occur.

Once your baby has worked up to three meals a day, and until they're about five, aim to give them:

- Lots of carbs – some at every meal

- Lots of fruit and veg – some at every meal and at least one green veg or orange fruit/veg per day

- Plenty of protein and iron – some at most meals and some oily fish each week

- Plenty of fats and oils – some every day

- Good amounts of full-fat dairy – some every day

- Not too much wholegrain

- Plenty of water to drink, in addition to milk

Quantities

Children vary in the amount they eat – some seem to eat as much as an adult, some seem to have the appetite of a bird, and many go between the two extremes. Just like adults, their calorific needs change, so it's impossible to be precise about the quantities you should give them. Offer what you think is enough, then be sensitive to your child's appetite. Young children listen to their bodies when it comes to deciding how much to eat – do what you can to help them retain that sensitivity. Give them several chances to eat each day – three meals and two snacks, say – and you're providing them with ample opportunity to get the nutrients they need.

Vegetarian and Vegan Diets

If you want to raise your baby on a vegetarian diet, it is important to plan meals very carefully. Since meat and fish are the richest and most easily absorbed sources of protein and iron, you need to make sure you're providing adequate alternatives.

Pulses, nuts, seeds, soy, grains, eggs and dairy products are good sources of protein. However, many non-meat proteins are 'incomplete'; i.e. they do not contain all the amino acids we need (see page 60). Dairy products and eggs are considered complete, as is the grain quinoa. Other sources of protein should be combined within the diet to create the right balance of amino acids. For example, you might mix beans or lentils with rice, serve pearl barley or spelt with a cheese sauce, or blend a nut butter into a yoghurt smoothie. You don't have to combine proteins at every meal, as long as there are lots of different protein sources within the diet as a whole.

Pulses, dried fruit, soya, green leafy veg, fortified breakfast cereals and eggs are all decent sources of iron, but should be combined with a vitamin-C rich food (almost any fruit or veg) to aid iron absorption.

To keep up their intake of calories, protein and calcium, vegetarian babies and toddlers need at least 500ml breastmilk or formula, or other dairy products, every day. Of course, if you're breastfeeding, you can't tell exactly how much they're getting – just feed on demand.

Raising a child on a vegan diet is a big commitment and some authorities advise against it. If it's what you intend to do, talk to your doctor – they should be able to refer you to a paediatric dietitian who can help you ensure your child is getting everything they need. There is no substitute for professional advice and a carefully thought-out nutritional plan.

If you're thinking about a vegan diet for your baby, consider the following:

- Vegan mothers need to pay particularly good attention to their own nutrition, from conception onwards, to help their baby lay down the stores of nutrients they need in utero.

- Breastfeeding is particularly important within the context of a vegan diet, not least as a source of calcium. Soya infant formula can be used but isn't recommended before 6 months. Ordinary soya milk is too low in fat for babies and may not be fortified with calcium. Calcium-containing veg such as spinach are great to include in the diet, but do not provide anywhere near enough calcium for a baby or small child.

- It can be very easy for a vegan diet not to contain enough calories for a growing child: plenty of fats and oils are important.

- The advice given above on non-animal sources of protein and iron in a vegetarian diet applies to vegans too.

- Vitamin B12, which is essential for growth, is only naturally available from animal products. You can buy B12-fortified products, such as yeast extract, but these tend to be salty, so a supplement may be better.

- Give a multi-vitamin supplement (suitable for vegans, of course).

Salt

I'm sure you know that eating too much salt is bad for you. Adults don't need much, children need even less, and babies' bodies cannot cope with any more than a tiny amount. Excessive quantities of salt can be extremely damaging to a child's body in the short term, but even a moderately high salt intake can lead in later life to high blood pressure, and thereby to heart disease and strokes. So, it's important to be very aware of sources of salt in your family's diet, and to keep consumption low.

I know parents who do not add a single grain of salt to any of the food they cook for their children. However, I'm not one of them. I don't think you have to ban salt altogether if you don't want to. Instead, I think we should all be shifting the balance away from eating convenience foods which are already high in salt, and towards eating home-made foods which we season, carefully, ourselves. As a nation, most of the salt we absorb comes from processed foods. If you prepare most of your own food from scratch, you have far greater control over the amounts of salt you and your family ingest – and, I think, you'll be likely to eat much less.

I wouldn't add any salt to food for babies under 1 year. Beyond that, and particularly if you are trying to include your child in family mealtimes,

AGE	SAFE AMOUNT OF SALT
Under 6 months	As provided by breast or formula milk only
6–12 months	Less than 1g salt per day
1–3 years	No more than 2g per day
4–6 years	No more than 3g salt per day
7–11 years	No more than 5g salt per day
Over 11 years	No more than 6g salt per day

I don't think there's anything wrong with adding a little salt to food as a seasoning. That is why you will find salt included as an optional ingredient in many of the recipes in this book. The point of seasoning is not to make food taste salty, only deliciously of itself. Always, always taste before you season – you might find salt is not necessary at all. But, personally, if I feel a sauce or soup needs a pinch to make it taste really good, I will go ahead and add it: after all, my children will only be eating a small portion of it.

My advice on salt is:

- Don't add salt to food for babies.

- Limit the amount of 'hidden' salt your children get by not giving them too many processed foods, such as ready-made sauces, pizzas, breakfast cereals and processed meats, such as ham and bacon. Keep a careful eye on child-friendly staples such as cheese, ready-made houmous, pesto and baked beans, which all contain a reasonable amount of salt.

- Be aware also that bread can contain a significant amount of salt. I don't think you should avoid bread – and if you make your own (see page 229), I think it tastes far better if you put salt in it – but it should only be one of a range of starchy carbs that your children eat. Include rice, oats, couscous, pasta and potatoes as well.

- Encourage the eating of potassium-rich foods (any fruit and veg, but particularly bananas, strawberries, grapes, dried fruit, leeks and greens), which help to balance out sodium in the body.

Many sources recommend using herbs and spices to flavour food 'instead of salt'. I don't think this is very helpful, as salt shouldn't be used to flavour food at all, but to enhance the flavour of other ingredients. Delicious as they are, herbs and spices don't mimic salt's unique seasoning action. But I'm all for keeping salt low. Among the things I've found helpful is adding garlic to a dish – the sweet intensity seems to season all kinds of savoury dishes, and children often love the flavour. A pinch of sugar in a savoury dish (not enough to make it taste sweet) can have a similar seasoning effect to salt too, especially in slightly acidic things such as tomato sauces.

Finally, when you're trying to keep salt to a minimum, make the most of 'umami' flavours. Umami is the fifth taste, along with sweet, sour, bitter and salty, and comes through in deeply savoury things such as well-browned meat, stocks, tomatoes, mushrooms and fish. Such foods are intensely flavoured in themselves and can enhance the flavour of other ingredients (interestingly, breastmilk is high in umami).

Sugar

Sugar can cause tooth decay and can contribute to obesity, if eaten to excess. Foods which are high in refined sugar and not much else can do horrible things to a child's blood sugar and thereby to their mood and behaviour. Refined sugar, on its own, has no nutritional value other than providing calories. However, it is, in my view, perfectly alright to give your children sugar sometimes. It's ok for them to eat some cake, the occasional pudding, the odd ice cream or biscuit. Certainly we should give sugar in moderation but that doesn't mean we have to eschew it altogether.

The way in which sugar is eaten is important. Refined sugar, by which I mean the beet or cane sugar (sucrose) that comes out of a packet, is essentially 'empty calories'. Eaten alone, it gives us a quick burst of energy, then quickly leaves us. Plastic sweeties (you know, the pick 'n' mix variety), fizzy drinks, chocolate bars and other foods that contain refined sugar and not much else are of no use nutritionally, and can affect children's mood and behaviour by giving them a shot of manic energy followed by a slump.

However, the energy sugar provides can be useful if it's combined with nutritious foods – such as fruit, dairy products, oats or eggs – which are filling, and release energy more slowly. Taking advantage of foods rich in 'natural' sugars, such as fructose (in fruit) or lactose (in milk) is a good idea. These sugars tend not to deliver energy into the bloodstream too quickly, and are often found in foods that bring all sorts of other valuable nutrients to the body. But I think sensible, restrained use of refined sugar can also be part of a balanced approach to cooking for children.

Sugar's knack of making things taste scrumptious should not be overlooked. It can sometimes function as a seasoning, rather than a main ingredient: a pinch or two can help to soften tart fruits or acidic sauces, for instance. However, there are, of course, other dishes – often the most coveted dishes of childhood – in which sugar is undeniably a major player. Cakes, biscuits, ice cream etc, all contain a lot of the sweet stuff. While these foods should definitely be given in small amounts, I believe that it's important not to ban them – or indeed any foods – from the family diet. Make something forbidden and you make it instantly more desirable. American studies have suggested that restricting access to certain foods can make young children more likely to eat those foods when they do get the opportunity.

As with salt, much of the general concern about sugar is focused on processed foods or those where the sugar is 'hidden' – fruit yoghurts, breakfast cereals, cereal bars etc. A home-made cake or biscuit can be a very different, and altogether more wholesome, prospect. Not only do you retain control over how much sugar goes into it – and you can use much less than a commercial recipe would – you're also likely to be using natural, unadulterated ingredients, which may well include fresh fruit and veg, organic flour, ground nuts, vegetable oils and eggs, rather than stabilisers, thickeners and preservatives.

I think it's unwise to present sweet sugary foods as treats, rewards or guilty secrets, eaten only on special occasions, or in response to 'good' behaviour, or when we think no one else is looking. All these approaches invest those foods with an allure that makes them stand out from other fare, makes them something to be sought out, devoured quickly before they can be taken away, maybe even hoarded or hidden. Ideally, I think, these foods just need to be present, some of the time, in moderate quantities – an enjoyable but unremarkable part of the family diet.

Sugar and teeth

When it comes to teeth, there is some difference between 'natural' sugars such as the fructose or lactose you would find in fruit or milk, and 'refined' sugars such as the sucrose and glucose you'd get in sweets. Sucrose is more likely to cause caries, and it often comes in a concentrated form in foods, like sweets, that will stick to the teeth. There's much less sugar in an apple than in a bag of jelly beans, and it's mitigated by the water in the fruit and its non-sticky texture.

However, natural sugar is still sugar, and bacteria in the mouth will feed on any sugar at all – even the sugars in vegetables or grains. I say this not to make you feel bad about feeding your child 'healthy' foods, but to make you feel ok about giving them sweet foods sometimes.

As I've suggested already, the way that sugar is consumed is significant. Prolonged or frequent contact with sugar is the real risk for teeth. One ice cream eaten in 10 minutes is far less damaging than a bottle of apple juice sucked over several hours. The mouth releases decay-causing acid for about 20 minutes after each sugar-eating episode. If the sugar-eating goes on and on, regardless of the actual quantity, the acid goes on and on too. This is why, regardless of what your child is eating, regular meals are better for the teeth than constant grazing. And it goes without saying that teeth-cleaning is always important.

Non-refined and 'natural' sugars

Try not to be too taken in by packets of 'raw' or 'unrefined' sugar. Don't get me wrong, I like these products. They are far less processed and more flavourful than pure white sugar, which is treated with chemicals and stripped of its natural molasses. But they're still straight sucrose and will have the same effects on teeth and energy levels. The same goes for 'brown' or demerara sugars; these are not somehow better for you than white sugar. Honey is another sweetener sometimes seen as 'healthy'. While it can be very pure and minimally processed – especially if you buy it from a small, local producer – and while it does contain trace amounts of some nutrients, it's still basically sugar.

My advice on sugar is:

- Be very cautious about adding sugar to food for babies (anyone under 12 months).

- Make sure sugar is always combined in small quantities with nutritious, sustaining ingredients. Do not give it on its own, or combined with not much else, or in large quantities (as with sweets, fizzy drinks, some juices or squashes, ready-made cakes and biscuits).

- For the sake of your children's teeth, give sweet foods as part of a meal rather than for grazing. Combine them with other, non-sugary foods – and clean those teeth as well as you feasibly can!

What Shouldn't You Give Them?

Over recent years, the advice on what babies and young children should and shouldn't eat, and when they should or shouldn't eat it, has been confusing. Although some foods should be given with caution because they carry a small risk of food poisoning or choking, the principal reason given for delaying the introduction of certain foods – or avoiding those foods altogether – is that they have been perceived as an allergy risk.

A great deal of analysis has been done in this area of late and the emerging consensus makes things simpler for parents: once your child reaches 6 months, you do not need to delay the introduction of allergenic foods, even if your family is allergy-prone. To quote the World Health Organisation, 'there are no controlled studies that show that restrictive diets have an allergy-preventing effect. Therefore young children can consume a variety of foods from the age of 6 months including cow's milk, eggs, peanuts, fish and shellfish'.

It is true that children who come from families with a history of allergies are still at a greater risk of developing them. If you suffer from food allergies, or know a child who has, you may find this approach alarmingly gung-ho after years of being told to hold back. But some researchers now believe that delaying the introduction of allergenic foods could actually increase the risk of allergic sensitisation. No one is saying potentially allergenic foods (listed overleaf) should be rushed into your baby's system all at once but they are no longer off the menu.

Unfortunately, with allergies, there are no guarantees. These distressing conditions will still occur in some children, even if you have no family history of allergies. It remains a very good idea to introduce these foods carefully, one at a time, and watch for any reaction. This is particularly true if your child has already been diagnosed with an allergic condition, such as eczema, or if you, your partner or other children suffer from allergies (including non-food allergies, such as hay fever). But the most up-to-date research suggests that avoiding foods is not a good way to prevent allergies from occurring. So, here's the hard-and-fast stuff:

AGE	AVOID GIVING	WHY
Under 6 months	It is generally not advised to give your baby any solids under 6 months and you should definitely not start before 4 months (see page 40). Under 6 months, the government tells us not to give nuts and seeds, eggs, cow's milk, soya, wheat, gluten, fish, shellfish, soft and unpasteurised cheeses, and liver	The government maintains there is still not clear evidence that giving potentially allergenic foods before 6 months is safe. Some of these foods also carry a small risk of food poisoning, the dangers of which are greater for a very young baby. Nuts can cause choking. Liver is very high in vitamin A
Under 12 months	Honey	This carries a small risk of infant botulism
	Added sugar (though small amounts of sugar used when cooking nutritious foods, such as fruit, are ok)	Can contribute to tooth decay and provides little nutrition
	Added salt (or very salty foods)	Babies' kidneys cannot cope with it
	Raw or lightly cooked eggs (fully cooked eggs are fine over 6 months)	Risk of food poisoning
Under 5 years	Raw shellfish	Risk of food poisoning
	Whole or chopped nuts or large seeds	Risk of choking
	Shark, swordfish, marlin	May contain high levels of mercury

Food allergies and intolerance

Certain foods, which are more strongly linked with allergy and food intolerance, should be introduced more cautiously. Offer these foods from 6 months, gradually, in small amounts, one by one, avoiding them only if your baby has an adverse reaction. Instant allergic reactions might be a rash, itching, swelling, vomiting, diarrhoea or breathing difficulties. Longer term effects, more indicative of an intolerance than an allergy, might include diarrhoea or constipation, wheezing, a runny nose or congestion.

The foods most often associated with allergy and intolerance are:

- Peanuts: If your child has already been diagnosed with another allergy, such as eczema, or there are allergies in your family, the government still advises that you talk to your doctor before introducing peanuts

- Tree nuts (brazils, hazelnuts, walnuts etc)

- Seeds

- Eggs

- Cow's milk

- Soya

- Wheat and other gluten-containing cereals, such as rye and barley, and oats, which contain a protein very similar to gluten

- Fish and shellfish

Other less common food allergens are celery, mustard seed and kiwi fruit. There are a few fruits you may have been told to be careful with, too, including citrus fruits, berries, tomatoes and pineapple. These are among a group of foods that can sometimes trigger 'oral allergy syndrome' – usually itching or swelling in or around the mouth. These symptoms are unlikely to spread to other parts of the body but are still unpleasant. If you are concerned, introduce these fruits in small quantities and, if you note any reaction, steer clear of the food. Pineapple also contains strong enzymes that can simply make the mouth sore.

   If your child does have a food allergy, there's a good chance they'll be free of it by the time they are in double figures. In fact, with the exception of nuts, most food allergies and intolerances are outgrown by school age.

Dairy allergy and intolerance

If a youngster in the UK is going to be intolerant or allergic to anything, it's most likely to be dairy products. Dairy allergy affects 2–7 per cent of babies under a year, though they are very likely to grow out of it by the time they're 3 years old. Symptoms can be severe, usually appear within 30 minutes of eating the food, and can include rashes, wheezing, vomiting, diarrhoea or breathing difficulties.

Dairy intolerance is more common. It's estimated that up to 25 per cent of young children experience it to varying degrees but, again, they often grow out of it. The symptoms are similar to allergy: skin problems, runny nose or congestion, diarrhoea or vomiting (but not breathing difficulties). Intolerance symptoms generally build up over several days rather than appearing immediately as with an allergy, and sometimes the child can tolerate a certain amount of the food before symptoms begin. If you're concerned that your child may be reacting badly to dairy products, speak to your health visitor or GP before making drastic changes to their diet.

If you do need to cut dairy out of your child's diet, don't panic. It's not hard to find good, dairy-free recipes and most others can be adapted. You can replace butter with olive or rapeseed oil, for instance, or use a dairy-free margarine on bread (check the label, most margarines are not actually dairy-free). Ripe avocado is a good substitute for butter or cheese in sandwiches, as is mayonnaise (made with pasteurised eggs, rather than home-made). On soups and vegetable or pasta dishes, use garlicky fried breadcrumbs or croûtons instead of cheese. Try calcium-fortified soya yoghurts and milks for children over 6 months.

'Isla had really bad reflux from birth. At about 3 months, it got even worse and she started losing weight. They thought it was an intolerance to cow's milk protein coming through in my breastmilk. So I went dairy-free, and that really helped – though it didn't stop the reflux altogether. We didn't give her any dairy foods when we started weaning her, but introduced them very gradually from around 10 months. She seems to have grown out of the intolerance and we don't have to restrict her diet now.'
Sharnie, mum to Isla, 14 months

Problems with Food

Dealing with conflict and anxiety at mealtimes

PARENTS HAVE an overwhelming desire to feed their children – it's natural, it's essential. And, as I've said, there are few things as deeply satisfying as cooking something nutritious for your son or daughter, sitting down with them and watching them eat it all up. It makes you feel whole as a parent, it makes you feel you're doing a good job, it makes you feel your love has been received with thanks. That's why it's so distressing when your child won't eat, or won't eat what you think are the right things.

If your child has an entirely happy relationship with food, readily eats a wide variety of nutritious things, and enjoys relaxed and pleasant family mealtimes in your company, then please skip this chapter. I am not saying this flippantly: I know there are children like that, and I don't want to start creating problems in parental minds where there are none. So, really, if it's all going well, please turn straight to the recipes and enjoy!

If, however, you and your child have food issues, whether few or many, I hope I can offer you support, at the very least, and perhaps some helpful information too.

'Beth doesn't go outside her comfort zone with food. She's not prepared to try new things. To be honest, my problem is her rejection of my authority. I'm not worried about her diet as such. I know she's getting enough nutrients and enough calories. It's about control – hers and mine. I want her to enjoy food in the same way I do.'
Katie, mum to Beth, 3

'Tilly spits things out sometimes, which I find really hard. I think, "How dare you! I cooked that!", but I try to be relaxed and not make an issue of it. They're never allowed to say that food is yukky, though, I won't have that.'
Mac, mum to Lex, 3, and Tilly, 1

Issues over Food

The problems parents most often struggle with are so-called 'picky eating', when a child won't accept the foods you've selected for them, and the refusal to eat much at all. Both can be immensely frustrating, worrying and distressing. Believe me. I know. I have struggled with both those issues at length. There is no magic answer, but you will save yourself and your children a lot of grief if you accept, early on, that you cannot control what they eat. You can only guide them: by providing the right sort of foods and by setting the right example of desirable eating behaviour.

Ellyn Satter, an American dietitian and family therapist, in her book, *Child of Mine*, says it is the parents' job to decide the what, when and where of feeding, while the child's job is to decide the whether and how much. She points out that children, from birth, know how much to eat in order to grow in the way nature intended, and that they retain that ability throughout life as long as no one interferes with it. We need to offer them varied and appealing meals, but then allow them to listen to their own hunger and appetite. According to Satter, you are not responsible for how much your child eats, nor the way their body develops. 'You must do your part in feeding by reliably and lovingly providing him with appropriate food. You must limit his sedentary activities and give him opportunities to be active... Once you have done all of that, you must trust the outcome.' It's a philosophy I've found to ring true, and to be very liberating.

Food refusal

It is often, though not exclusively, the case that a child will be very open to trying lots of different foods in the first few months of weaning then, some time between 12 and 24 months, everything will change. They might refuse to try anything new, they might refuse foods they previously ate happily and they might become very contrary – eating peas or chicken one day, then refusing them for weeks, or only eating toast if it's cut in triangles rather than squares. This is a perfectly normal developmental stage. It's called neophobia ('fear of the new') and has been documented by various researchers studying children's eating habits. The theory is that this phase evolved to help protect a curious and newly mobile child from eating harmful or poisonous things. So if it seems that your toddler is treating unfamiliar food with outright suspicion, as if they think you might be trying to poison them, it's probably because that is exactly what they're thinking!

Dr Gillian Harris, Consultant Paediatric Clinical Psychologist at the Children's Hospital, Birmingham, says: 'At roughly 18 months, children begin to adhere to rigid visual prototypes – which means they don't eat anything that doesn't look right. So tomatoes might be fine, but tomato sauce is not. It may even be the case that tomato sauce was fine last week, but today it looks different, so it's not fine anymore. During this phase it's best to feed your child things they are comfortable with, but continue to expose them to other foods and eat them yourself (so they learn that they're not poisonous). Don't pressure them to try new foods if they don't want to or you will begin to create anxiety around mealtimes. Anxiety increases adrenaline and adrenaline decreases appetite.'

With this in mind, I don't think it's helpful to use the term 'picky eater', because it has such negative connotations. A child who won't eat the dinner you've carefully prepared for them may seem pedantic, difficult to please, awkward and frankly rather rude, but a great deal of this 'fussiness' stems from that fear of the unfamiliar, from neophobia. So rather than 'picky', a child who is very reluctant to eat something could be better described as under-confident, unsure, even afraid. And when you look at it like that, you can see that what they need is not pressure, threats and ultimatums, but reassurance, help and encouragement.

It's also my belief that small children use mealtimes to find out more about their own place in the world and their influence on the people around them. Once a child realises that they can say no to food or that they can get a reaction if they make a fuss, they will naturally explore the situation. Dietitian Judy More makes a very good point about this in her book, *Feeding Your Baby*: 'Parents tend to become more anxious when a baby refuses food than when he won't wear a hat or socks. But to the baby, it's all just part of the same game.' And a friend of mine made a similar point: 'Food is the one thing they have some control over, isn't it? You can physically make them sit in their car seat, or move away from the television, but you can't force them to put something in their mouth.'

Not eating enough

It is normal for babies and toddlers to have inconsistent eating patterns. They might go for a few days eating very little, then seem to be starving all the time. Others seem to survive on an extraordinarily small amount of food. They may go through fads, focusing on just one or two foods for a period of time, then rejecting them in favour of something quite different.

Young children eat according to their appetite rather than by routine and habit, as adults may. This can vary a lot, especially after the first year: growth slows down then, so their daily activity has more of a direct effect on how hungry they are. I think it is important to allow children to eat according to their appetite, and not try to over-ride it. Eating when you're not hungry doesn't generally make anyone feel good.

There is evidence to suggest that young children – even babies – know how much they need to eat. Back in the 1930s, an American doctor, Clara Davis, studied babies' ability to self-select their own meals from a broad selection of unprocessed wholefoods, including fruit, vegetables, milk, cereals, meat, fish, offal and water. While each child consumed a different diet, all were exceptionally healthy, consumed the right amount of calories and selected a combination of foods that seemed to ensure a good intake of protein, vitamins and minerals. Adults should decide which foods are made available, Davis concluded, but within that, a child whose appetite is allowed to 'function freely', can absolutely thrive.

More recently, Leann Birch and Jennifer Fisher, US scientists who study the way children eat, have shown that youngsters can instinctively adapt their calorie intake according to how much they've already consumed. In addition, they say that while energy intake at different meals can vary considerably, total daily energy intake may well be pretty consistent.

None of this means you should stop trying to feed your child the very best you can – Birch and Fisher point out, like Davis, that the range of foods on offer still needs to be 'healthful' – it just means you don't have to panic every time they fail to eat what you think is a good meal.

How to deal with anxiety when a child won't eat what you want them to:

- Do not equate rejection of food with rejection of love, even though that's what it feels like sometimes.

- Make a mental list of everything they have eaten over the last week or so. You may discover that it actually represents a reasonable quantity and quite a balanced diet to boot. Even if the number of different ingredients is limited, they're probably getting all the major food groups (i.e. toast, yoghurt, banana and fishfingers isn't a bad range, nutritionally speaking).

- Comfort yourself with the thought that many a food-shy toddler has bloomed, in adulthood, into a veritable gourmand.

- Focus on the atmosphere of the meal, not the substance – if everyone is having a calm and pleasant eating experience, then you have achieved something very important.

- Remember that sometimes your child may not be eating much for a physical reason rather than a psychological one. If their food refusal seems out of character, run through a quick checklist: are they tired, anxious, grumpy, over-stimulated or trying to deal with a new situation or unfamiliar people? Are they teething? Could they be coming down with a cold or a bug? Could there be a more serious underlying health problem that decreases appetite, such as anaemia? If your child doesn't eat much iron-rich food (see page 62), and is also lethargic and prone to illness, it could be worth asking your doctor to test for anaemia.

Eating too much

What if you think your child is eating too much? What if you think they're overweight? This is a very difficult area, about which mothers in particular can have complex and painful feelings. Anyone who's ever had concerns about their own weight can feel a horrible mixture of guilt, anxiety and confusion if they perceive their child to be 'greedy' or 'fat'. And aren't we told constantly that we're raising a generation of obese youngsters?

If you're worried that your child is seriously overweight, you should seek professional advice. But I believe it's often better to offer a balanced diet and let children regulate their own intake, than to intervene and begin to create anxiety, guilt and negative associations around food. There is research that backs this up. Birch and Fisher, again, say that a high degree of parental control when it comes to eating is associated with greater fatness in children; i.e. those youngsters do not learn to self-regulate.

Anyone who's been on a diet will know how counter-productive and miserable it can be to deny yourself food. Keep your children active. Turn off the TV and take them to the park, swimming pool or soft play centre. Encourage them to be strong, fit and healthy. Offer a range of healthy foods, but don't ban anything. Cakes, biscuits and chocolate shouldn't be seen as forbidden, ultra-desirable treats or rewards – just make sure they are not available all the time. You have to accept that some children are skinny and some are chubby – you can't do a lot to change that and it doesn't necessarily mean they will grow into skinny or chubby adults. Guide them towards an active, healthy lifestyle but accept them as they are.

How to Cope with Difficult Mealtimes

If a child is going through a tricky eating phase, it may well pass after a few months. But while the pattern of being open to new foods, then closing in, then opening up again applies to many children, it doesn't fit all of them. Some are funny about food from the word go and never really seem to enjoy it. Some start off quite uninterested, then gradually bloom into omnivores. Some never eat very much, some seem to eat an awful lot. They are all different and you have to find a strategy for managing mealtimes in your own family that works for you. However, two principles that doctors, dietitians and experienced parents universally agree on are:

Keep trying Keep offering the foods that you want them to eat, over and over again. Don't fall into the: 'It's not worth it, they'll never eat it' trap. Repetition allows your child to become familiar with the food – even if they don't eat it. A tiny taste, or just tolerating it on their plate, is a step in the right direction. A child may need to taste a food many times before they build up the confidence they need to actually eat it.

Show the way Eat the foods you want your child to eat, and let them see you doing so. This won't necessarily bring instant results. Gently explaining that fish is a scrumptious food that you love may leave them unmoved. However, presenting that food regularly, in various tasty ways, and eating it with evident but understated enjoyment yourself sends the right message: 'This is good, this is normal, you don't have to be afraid of this.'

You can't necessarily stop food-related problems from arising – often, they are linked to your child's age, temperament, appetite and tastes, none of which you can affect. What's important is how you deal with issues when they do come up. Things can go either way. Mealtimes can spiral into a state of conflict, distress and misery, or, with great effort and self-control on your part, they can remain calm and pleasant while your child navigates this developmental stage. Here are some thoughts on avoiding conflict and fostering the best possible attitudes to food that you can:

Remain calm This is hard. I mean really hard, but you've got to aim for it. Scolding, shouting, crying, stamping around, ostentatiously throwing food in the bin while you hiss, 'Why do I bother?' – in short, any interesting behaviour on your part – is an irresistible bait to your child. They have a powerful, 'What happens when I push this button?' urge. But, if nothing happens, they'll move onto the next thing. Leave the room for a minute if you can, and ask another responsible adult to take over.

Don't hover over them Share their meal, eating the same thing yourself, if you possibly can. If you can't, I've come to believe that it is often better not to sit at the table at all, but to do something else nearby and let them get on with it. The worst thing you can do, if you're having any kind of issues with food, is to sit at the table, not eating anything yourself but staring pointedly at your child's plate, watching every morsel they eat. Would you enjoy eating in that way?

Don't bribe, cajole or force them to eat more or less than they want to It's counter-productive to do so. If they don't want to eat any more porridge, stew or apple purée, nothing you can do or say will change that. Either you have a battle on your hands, or they'll eat it under duress, which creates negative associations with food and with mealtimes. Let your child choose how much to eat. This enables them to be sensitive to their own appetite.

Recognise when they've had enough Even pre-verbal babies can show you when they're full: they may turn their head away, push the bowl away, repeatedly spit out food, hold food in the mouth without swallowing it, or make a fuss. Respond to their signals, not your idea of what's 'enough'.

Don't offer endless choice If your child refuses food, you may feel anxious. Will they last through the night? It's wise to include some element in a meal that you think they'll enjoy, but if they reject what's on offer, you don't have to rustle up something else. If you always respond by presenting their favourite snacks, they might think they don't need to try anything new, or eat anything they don't love, because something familiar and safe will be provided instead. It can be scary to let your child leave the table under-fed, but there will soon be another opportunity for them to eat.

Don't deceive them Don't hide new foods under familiar ones or trick them by putting something new inside a 'safe' container, such as a pot that usually contains their favourite yoghurt. It doesn't foster confidence and could put them off both the new food and the familiar one.

Set a time limit for meals If they're going to eat, the chances are they will do it in the first 20 minutes or so. Meals that last longer than 30 minutes are probably going nowhere and everyone will get bored and frustrated.

Don't make food into a reward If you say 'you can't have a chocolate biscuit until you eat your cauliflower cheese', you're implying that the biscuit is special, and the cauliflower is a trial. If the biscuits were on the menu for this particular meal, give them anyway, whether the cauliflower gets eaten or not. Don't give 'treats' such as sweets or cake as rewards for good behaviour; again, you are making those foods seem ultra-desirable.

Take the long view Right now you may be trying to get a balanced meal into the little tinker, but you're also doing your best to set them up for a lifetime of good eating, a happy and healthy relationship with food. Pick your battles and look for alternatives. Can you let the broccoli go for now and serve up a fruit salad (which has many of the same nutrients) later?

Grow, shop and cook with them Getting your children involved in bringing a meal to the table is a good way to make them feel more comfortable with it, more interested in it and more in control of the whole eating thing. On page 99 I've listed some of the many ways that even a toddler can get cooking. It is also generally true that children who've been involved with growing or gathering fruit and veg are more likely to try them.

Encouraging Your Child to Eat Well

Eating well is more than a case of ingesting the right nutrients. It's about being open to trying a range of good things, enjoying mealtimes and being relaxed about food, being able to eat when hungry and stop when full. Achieving this is an ongoing process. If you're in a difficult phase and mealtimes are not going well, step back a little. Ask yourself if you're offering good nutritious, tasty, fresh and varied food. If the answer is yes, then try to relax. Your child has the wherewithal to eat well, to get what they need, but they have to deal with all the challenges of growing up at the same time. Make the right food available, make it appealing, then leave it up to them. This is the hardest part of all. Because as well as loving your child, which is easy, you've got to trust them, which sometimes, is not.

2. RECIPES

Cooking for the Family

A flexible approach

THIS BOOK is about feeding children, but these recipes are intended for adults too. I don't think there should be any sharp distinctions between 'baby food', 'children's food' and 'grown-up food'. There may be a sliding scale – with, at the most junior end, food that is simpler and less demanding to eat – but it's a spectrum the whole family should be able to enjoy, the food each person eats becoming just a little more sophisticated and perhaps more seasoned as they mature.

These recipes are arranged seasonally, so you can take advantage of the ingredients that should be freshest and best at any given time (though several are good all-year-rounders). I've made the dishes as nutritionally balanced as possible, or suggested things to serve them with that will provide a balanced meal. And I've tried to keep things simple, with short ingredient lists and straightforward techniques. Almost all the recipes are adaptable – do not hesitate to change some of the ingredients, depending on what you have or what you like. If you're happy making a white sauce for the pasta bake on page 210, for instance, you can use the same sauce with all sorts of other pasta or vegetable dishes.

Servings

It's hard to define what a child's portion size should be. In order to give a useful idea of how much each recipe makes, and reflecting the fact that these are intended for the whole family, I've given serving sizes in terms of adult portions. Many of the recipes serve three adults because this is a useful quantity if you are serving a family of two grown-ups and two small children. If, however, it's a recipe that freezes well, I'll often make it in larger quantities. Sometimes the nature of the ingredients (a whole chicken, for instance) dictates how much the recipe makes.

Ages

I have tried to provide you here with recipes that all the family can eat, even if that means simplifying them slightly for babies, or augmenting them for adult tastes. There are notes on the recipes to show you what I mean. Where I've referred to 'babies' in general, I mean 6–12 month olds, but where I say 'young babies', I mean roughly 6–9 month olds, i.e. those who may still struggle with some textures. When I say 'older children', I'm thinking of those aged five and upwards.

With the exception of the purées, all the recipes are aimed at babies of 6 months and upwards; i.e. they include ingredients such as cow's milk, eggs and fish, which are not advised for younger babies.

Notes on Ingredients

I've talked quite a bit about selecting good foods in the previous chapter, but here are some notes on specific ingredients that explain some of my choices in more detail.

Apples and apple juice

I make no apology for my fond reliance on apples and good-quality apple juice. Not only are apples wonderfully good for you, they are also a fantastic British food. Available for more than half of the year, they are delicious and incredibly versatile. The range of British apples available is increasing all the time, and it's really worth trying different varieties if you can source them. For further information on different apple varieties, visit www.commonground.org.uk.

I've avoided using cooking apples such as Bramleys here, because you need to add a reasonable amount of sugar to them. Instead, I favour dessert apples such as Discovery, Early Windsor, Cox's Orange Pippin, Orleans Reinette and Egremont Russet.

Apple juice is a wonderful ingredient when you're cooking for kids too, enabling you to sweeten many dishes without adding refined sugar. When I list apple juice in a recipe, I mean pure, fresh-pressed, cloudy juice – the sort you can get from any decent farm shop – not from concentrate. Some shops sell single-variety juices and I find the particularly sweet ones, such as Russet or Elstar, are very useful in cooking.

Cheese

I've been deliberately non-specific about varieties of cheese in many of these recipes because there are so many wonderful different British types available, often exclusive to certain regions. Even if I've listed something by name, such as Cheddar, feel free to substitute something else. Any firm, flavoursome, meltable cheese will work in a sauce, or sprinkled on soup or grilled on a frittata. Try gorgeous Cornish Yarg or smooth Berkswell, delicately tangy sheep's milk Wensleydale, or creamy and robust Suffolk Shipcord (my local favourite). You can also get excellent British buffalo mozzarella now. I'm rather attached to good Italian Parmesan, but if I can get hold of a British alternative, such as the mature, hard Dorset goat's cheese, Capriano, I use it.

Parents sometimes feel unsure about giving certain types of cheese to children because of fears of food poisoning. The issue here is not to do with pasteurisation or lack of it – pasteurisation doesn't guarantee that a cheese is 'safe', because the milk or cheese can be contaminated at a later stage. However, there are some cheeses which, pasteurised or not, are more likely to harbour high levels of listeria. The key factors are the acidity and moisture level of the cheese itself.

Cheeses which carry a greater risk are soft, mould-ripened types such as camembert, brie and others with a similar 'mouldy' rind, as well as mould-ripened soft goat's cheeses such as chèvre, and soft blue cheeses. As it's difficult to define a 'soft' blue cheese – Stilton is not exactly hard – I group all blue cheese in this category, to be on the safe side.

The people who really need to be aware of the risk from such cheeses are pregnant women because listeria can make them very ill, and may harm their unborn child. Those with compromised immune systems are also at greater risk. But listeria infection in healthy adults and children is rare.

Hard cheeses (even if unpasteurised), processed cheeses, cream cheese, cottage cheese, and fresh, unrinded goat's cheese, are not considered to carry a significant listeria risk. Note that cooking will destroy listeria.

Cooking oils and fats

In general, I prefer to use unrefined oils for cooking. For most sautéing, shallow-frying and roasting, I use rapeseed or olive oil.

Rapeseed oil This is a wonderful homegrown alternative to olive oil. Go for a virgin, cold-pressed British rapeseed oil, which will be very different to the highly refined rapeseed or 'canola' oil that often goes into anonymous 'vegetable' oils. Virgin rapeseed is more nutty, sweet and delicate than olive oil and ideal in dressings and even cakes. It is also a particularly good source of omega-3 essential fatty acids, and vitamin E.

Olive oil I usually choose an inexpensive, not-too-strongly flavoured extra virgin olive oil. Olive oil is naturally high in 'healthy' monounsaturated fats, which also makes it relatively stable when heated (though I wouldn't use it for deep-frying). I also love the rich, fruity flavour.

Sunflower oil Sometimes, I want a cooking oil that contributes no flavour at all to the finished dish, and sunflower is my choice. Most sunflower oils are quite heavily refined, and often treated with solvents and bleaches. I like Clearspring's Organic Sunflower Frying Oil – it is treated with steam to make it neutral in flavour, and comes from a specific type of sunflower seed higher in monounsaturated fats, which means it can be safely heated to higher temperatures than standard sunflower oil.

Butter Unsalted butter is lovely to cook with as it gives such a wonderful flavour, but it burns fairly easily. So, if you fry with it, always add a dash of oil too, to stop burning. Salted butter has an even lower burn point and, obviously, contains salt, so I don't cook with it.

Dried fruit

I use a lot of dried fruit and I buy organic, if at all possible, as conventional dried fruit often contains preservatives. Non-organic dried apricots, in particular, are routinely treated with sulphur dioxide to preserve a bright orange colour.

Nut butters

Smooth butters – made from peanuts, almonds, cashews, hazelnuts or other nuts – are a delicious and simple way to add protein and calories to a child's diet, provided, of course, nut allergy isn't an issue. Avoid the crunchy varieties as small pieces of nut can be a choking risk. Many nut butters contain a significant amount of added sugar and salt, so always check the label. A healthfood shop is likely to be your best bet for sugar- and salt-free nut butters. My favourite is cashew, which has a lovely natural sweetness.

Spelt

This is an ancient type of wheat, currently enjoying a renaissance, as some
people find it easier to digest than modern wheats. It's also deliciously
nutty-tasting. You can buy unrefined, wholegrain spelt flour, which I often
use instead of standard wholemeal flour in cakes or bread, and a refined
'white' version, which is good for lighter baking. Pearled spelt, similar
to pearl barley, is also lovely and a handy alternative to potatoes, rice
or pasta.

Seasoning

In most savoury recipes, I list salt and pepper as optional ingredients. I do
add a little finely ground pepper to most family food. However, it's best
not to add any salt to food for babies of 12 months or younger. Beyond
that, whether you use a little salt or not is up to you. For more on safe
quantities of salt, see pages 68–9.

Spices and chilli

There is no reason to exclude these. Introduce chilli very cautiously to
babies, and don't go mad even with older children – it is, after all, an
irritant – but don't assume your child won't like it. Where I've used chilli
in a recipe I've erred on the cautious side. Most of the heat is contained in
the seeds and membranes so, by removing these, you do a lot to tame the
chilli's heat. Feel free to alter the chilli content to suit your family's tastes.

Stock

I cannot overstate the wonderful, flavour-giving, wholesome usefulness
of a good home-made stock when you're cooking simple family recipes
like the ones on the following pages. It will make your purées, soups,
stews, curries and risottos that much better, and is particularly important
for giving a good flavour base when you're using little or no salt.

You'll find simple recipes for chicken and vegetable stocks on pages
236–8), while the lamb recipe on page 218 produces a very tasty stock
as a kind of by-product too. If you don't have time to make your own
stock, you can buy very good, fresh, liquid chicken stocks (I prefer the
organic ones), but they are expensive. Stock cubes and granules can stand
in, but they never give the same fresh flavour and can be very salty.
Always look for low-salt versions.

Basic Hygiene

Food hygiene is always important, of course, but particularly so when you're cooking for babies and young children. There is no need to panic, just be conscientious.

- Always wash and dry your hands before cooking and make sure your kitchen surfaces, utensils and fridge are clean.

- Wash kitchen cloths and tea towels very frequently.

- In general, either very cold or very hot is good: store perishable foods in the fridge at 0–5°C (use a fridge thermometer), and cook or reheat things until piping hot (steaming, too hot to touch comfortably) all the way through. Bacteria generally don't like intense heat or cold. They tend to multiply most in warm conditions so don't leave food hanging about at room temperature, especially in hot weather, or allow things to warm up a little, cool down a little, warm up a little etc.

- Don't reheat food more than once.

- Once something is defrosted from the freezer, don't refreeze it unless it's been cooked first; i.e. you might defrost raw chicken, cook it into a curry, then freeze the curry.

- Keep cold places cold: don't put warm food in the fridge or freezer – cool it down first, as quickly as possible. Don't leave fridge or freezer doors open.

- Keep cooked and raw food separate. In the fridge, put raw meat or fish in a sealed container on the lowest shelf (I reserve a salad drawer for raw meat and wash it regularly) so no raw juices can drip onto other foods. Keep cooked or ready-to-eat foods higher up in the fridge.

- Wash your hands directly after handling raw meat and poultry, and wash utensils that come into contact with it thoroughly. Keep a separate chopping board specifically for preparing raw meat and fish, and don't use it for anything else. An inexpensive plastic board that can go in the dishwasher is ideal.

- Wash fruit and veg that's to be eaten raw.

Finding the Time to Cook

When you have a young family it can, at times, seem impossible to find time to cook. There are no easy solutions, but there is a general approach which can help. I call it knock-on cooking. What I mean by that is never viewing one meal as a self-contained entity, but always looking for a way in which it can have a knock-on effect to another meal – without more work. It's often straightforward to cook or prepare more than you need. This can be frozen or saved to form the basis of another meal. For instance:

- When you're having jacket spuds, bake an extra potato or two – then you've got potato to be mashed for fishcakes, cubed for frittata, or cut into wedges, tossed in oil and browned in a hot oven for chunky chips.

- Cook more fish than you need. Cooled then refrigerated, the excess can go into salads, fishcakes or recipes like the egg parcels (on page 180).

- The washing, trimming, peeling and chopping of fruit and vegetables is one of the more time-consuming and unavoidable elements of cooking. But you can save time if you prepare more than you need. Slice four carrots instead of two, for instance, and you've got the beginnings of tomorrow's soup. Fry two onions instead of one and you have the basis for an extra sauce/stir-fry/batch of burgers. If you then freeze that prepared veg, it will retain more nutrients. You can also save time, sometimes, by using a food processor to grate or mince vegetables, particularly if the finished dish is to be puréed.

- Cook big batches of purées from time to time and freeze in portions. Once defrosted, fruity purées make instant puds with yoghurt, or the basis of a cobbler or crumble (freeze the crumble topping too). Veggie purées can be turned pretty instantly into a soup or even a pasta sauce.

- Always turn stale bread and abandoned crusts into breadcrumbs, and freeze. Breadcrumbs never fail to come in handy.

- If you're making bread dough, make a lot – excess can be frozen before or after baking (see page 229).

- Recipes can often be broken down into elements that you can prepare throughout the day – this is particularly true of things which go into the oven for a final baking, such as crumbles, pasta bakes or gratins.

Cooking with your Kids

Getting your children involved with food preparation, from a very early age, is a win-win deal all round. On one level, cooking is tremendous fun for a toddler – akin to making sandcastles or squidging play-dough. But even while they're having a whale of a time dusting the entire kitchen with flour, they're learning about cooking. They're also, crucially, gaining confidence with food, peeling away some of the apprehension that can attach to new or unfamiliar ingredients. I think even very tiny toddlers can begin to get involved with preparing food (with appropriate supervision, of course), and that every time they do, it's of enormous value.

From as young as 18 months children can manage these tasks:

- Podding peas
- Washing fruit and veg in the sink or a bowl on the floor
- Snapping the ends off asparagus spears
- Peeling the husks off cobs of corn
- Mixing dry ingredients in a bowl
- Squashing strawberries or raspberries, for a purée or sauce
- Sprinkling – oats or seeds onto bread, for instance

And once they hit 3 years, with some assistance, they can try:

- Rubbing butter into flour (for pastry)
- Breaking and whisking eggs
- Kneading dough
- Rolling and cutting out pastry or dough
- Slicing soft ingredients such as bananas with a fairly blunt knife
- Trickling oil onto a salad
- Stirring batters, doughs and other mixtures
- Squeezing citrus fruit
- Grating cheese

Purées

First foods for your baby

IF YOU INTEND to start your baby off with spoon-feeding, this is a useful guide to preparing some of the fruit and veg they might enjoy in the early days. I hope the ideas will give you the confidence to start whizzing and blending away at home, rather than scouring the baby-food aisle in your local supermarket. However, you probably won't – in fact you probably shouldn't – purée your way through all this lot.

Puréeing is not a set stage, written in law, that you have to go through for a fixed number of weeks. Some parents are very happy not to serve purées at all, others find they form the basis of a baby's diet for months. Purées can also be integrated into a baby-led weaning strategy (see page 45). But in all cases they are really only a starting point, a stepping stone on the way to 'proper' food. It's really important to get your baby used to textured food and finger foods, and to encourage them to chew and move food around their mouths, as soon as they're ready.

Try some of the simple one-ingredient purées on pages 105–7, then when your baby is happy with those, take a look at the slightly more complex purée recipes on pages 107–13.

Playing Safe with Purées

You really don't have to don a white coat and a hairnet when you are making your own baby purées, but it does pay to be particularly mindful of food safety and hygiene. This is partly because little babies' immune systems are not 100 per cent mature so they are rather more susceptible to bugs, and food poisoning can be extremely serious for them. It's also because when you peel, cut up and purée food, you increase its surface area, and that creates more opportunities for bacteria to feed and grow. Don't let this put you off – just remember to take into account a few basics.

Food safety guidelines for preparing purées:

● Once completely cooled, cooked purées can be kept in the fridge for 24 hours, or frozen. Freeze them in small portions. An ice cube tray is the classic baby-purée holder, but I actually prefer a flexible silicone mini-muffin mould (shown opposite). These moulds are ideal for one-serving portions, and it's very easy to pop the frozen purée out. Defrost purées in the fridge, then reheat until piping hot and cool down before serving. Only reheat a purée once.

● There are a few purées here that are made with raw fruit and these I do not suggest freezing. This is because, once defrosted, they should really then be heated until piping hot, which simply wouldn't be very nice. Fresh fruit purées can easily be shared between the whole family so there shouldn't be any wastage.

● Many fruit and veg need to have a liquid added to them before they will blend to a smooth purée. You can use breast or formula milk, and these have the advantage of bringing calories and extra nutrients to the mix. However, if you're going to chill or freeze and reheat a purée, milk is not an ideal addition due to hygiene considerations. Home-made, unsalted stock is good for thinning savoury purées (though bear in mind that it will contain traces of lots of different ingredients). Again, if it's been cooked, chilled and reheated before being added to your purée, it's not then a good idea to chill/freeze and reheat it again. So use freshly made, still-hot stock for a purée that's to be frozen. For purées that you're not serving immediately, water is the simplest liquid to go for – use the water the ingredients were cooked with, if you can, as it will have absorbed some of their vitamins. Keep purées for freezing quite thick and you can add a little fresh milk or freshly made hot stock when the purée has been defrosted and reheated.

If you are going to do any amount of puréeing, it's really worthwhile investing in a good free-standing jug blender – they start from about £30. Hand-held 'stick' blenders are very useful for smooth soups or blitzing other 'wet' mixtures, but they don't always cope efficiently with thicker, chunkier blends.

For Starters: One-ingredient Purées

These simple home-made purées are a good way to start your baby off on the great food adventure.

Apple or pear
I always steam these: it preserves nutrients and you get a thicker, more intense purée than if you cook the fruit in water. Peel, core and slice 2 or 3 medium dessert apples or pears. Put in a steamer basket or a fine sieve balanced over a pan of simmering water. Cover and steam for 6–8 minutes, stirring once or twice, until soft. Purée. Makes 250–350ml.

Apricot
Steaming apricots in a sieve is an easy way to deal with the skins (you can do the same with a couple of peaches). Halve 4–5 apricots and remove the stones. Place flesh-side down in a fine sieve, so the halves don't overlap. Put over a pan of simmering water. Cover and steam for 5 minutes or so, until soft. Lift the sieve from the pan and use a spoon to rub the apricot flesh through the sieve into a bowl (discard the skins). Makes about 100ml.

Beetroot
Trim and scrub 2 medium beetroot (about 350g) under cold running water. Wrap them loosely in foil and bake at 190°C/gas 5 until really tender, 1–2 hours. When cool enough to handle, remove the skins with a small knife. Chop the beetroot roughly, then purée in a blender with enough water to get a smooth purée. Makes around 300ml.

Broccoli
Trim a head of broccoli, or bunch of purple sprouting broccoli, of fibrous stalks. Cut the tender tips into small pieces. Put in a steamer basket over a pan of simmering water. Steam for about 8 minutes, until tender. Purée with a little water until smooth. 150g trimmed broccoli yields about 200ml.

Cauliflower
Cut ¼ cauliflower (about 250g untrimmed) into small florets, then put in a steamer basket or a fine sieve over a pan of boiling water. Cover and steam for about 10 minutes, until tender, then purée with some of the steaming water. Makes about 200ml.

Pea

Bring a pan of water to the boil. Drop in 200g fresh or frozen peas (or petits pois). Return to a simmer and cook until tender – around 5 minutes for frozen peas, probably longer for fresh ones. Drain, saving the water. Transfer the peas to a blender and blend with enough of the cooking water to achieve the consistency you require. If you want a super-smooth pea purée for a very young baby, push the blended purée through a sieve. Makes around 300ml (unsieved).

Plum

Quarter about 500g plums, discard the stones and put the fruit into a saucepan with 1–2 tbsp water – just enough to stop them catching on the pan. Place over a low heat until the juices start to run, then bring slowly to a simmer and cook gently for about 15 minutes, stirring and crushing the fruit from time to time, until really soft. Purée the fruit, then return to the pan and put back on the heat. Increase the heat a little and simmer briskly, stirring from time to time so it doesn't burn, for about 10 minutes, until reduced by about a third. This thickens and intensifies the purée. If your baby is over 6 months, try mixing this with plain, full-fat yoghurt. Makes about 250ml.

Potato

Potatoes don't respond well to whizzing in a blender or food processor – they tend to develop a gluey texture. A few bits of potato in a purée with other ingredients will be fine but if you just want potato on its own, it's better to mash it. Peel the potato, cut into large chunks and boil for 15–20 minutes until tender, then drain well. Or bake your spuds (for about 1 hour at 200°C/gas 6) and scoop the flesh from the skin. Either way, mash the potato flesh with a fork, adding a little breast or formula milk or, if your baby is over 6 months, cow's milk and/or butter just before serving. A large potato yields around 200ml mash.

Root veg (carrot, celeriac, parsnip, swede, salsify)

Use these alone or in combination. Peel, slice, then steam until tender, about 15–20 minutes, then purée in a blender with a little of the steaming water. If you're using parsnips, make sure you remove all the woody core. You could also boil these veg, drain, then purée with a little of the cooking water. 350g root veg yields about 250ml purée.

Squash or pumpkin

Slice in half or quarters and scoop out the seeds. Put, cut side up, in an ovenproof dish. Pour half a glass of water into the dish. Cover loosely with foil and roast at 190°C/gas 5 until completely tender – 45 minutes–1 hour, but it depends on size and variety. Scoop the flesh from the skins and mash or purée, with liquid if needed. A butternut squash half yields about 300ml.

Sweet potato

Bake 2 medium sweet potatoes at 190°C/gas 5 for 45 minutes–1 hour, until completely tender. Slice them in half, scoop out the soft flesh with a teaspoon, then purée it. Two medium sweet potatoes yield about 200ml.

Moving On: Mixed Purées

Once those first purées are going down well, move on to mixed purées like these, adapting the texture to suit your baby. As they mature, make the purées thicker, and turn them into more substantial meals by adding other ingredients containing protein, carbohydrate or fat. Do this fairly swiftly if your baby is 6 months old or older. It's then a short stride to offering your baby normal family foods, chopped or mashed to a texture that suits them.

Veg-based purées

As soon as your baby seems ready, make these purées more textured by chopping or mashing the ingredients rather than liquidising them. To make any of them more substantial, try the following:

- If your baby is over 6 months, add grated cheese, a dash of cream, butter or plain, full-fat yoghurt before serving.

- If your baby is over 6 months, add chopped, well-cooked egg.

- Add some finely chopped, freshly cooked chicken (see page 109 or 236), lamb (see page 218) or fish (see page 239).

- If you're cooking the veg in a pan with water, add some red lentils at the start of cooking.

- Add some carbohydrate by cooking rice or pasta along with the veg, or crumbling bread into the mix.

Parsnip & apple

Peel, trim and quarter 2 medium parsnips, then cut out any woody core. Roughly chop the parsnips. Peel, core and roughly chop 4 medium dessert apples. Put the apples in a small pan with the parsnips and add enough water to half-cover the fruit and veg. Bring to the boil, cover, reduce the heat and simmer, stirring once or twice, for 6–8 minutes, until tender. Tip the pan contents into a blender and purée. Thin down individual portions just before serving with milk or hot stock if necessary. Makes about 400ml.

Carrot & cauliflower

Trim and roughly chop ½ medium cauliflower. Peel, trim and roughly chop 1 large carrot. Combine the veg in a steamer, or a fine sieve balanced over a pan of simmering water. Cover and steam for 10–15 minutes until soft. Transfer to a blender and purée with a little of the steaming water. Thin down individual portions just before serving with milk or hot stock if necessary. Makes about 300ml.

Broccoli, potato & fish

Bake 1 medium potato at 200°C/gas 6 for around 1 hour, until completely tender. Towards the end of the cooking time, place 1 small fish fillet (such as pollack or mackerel) on a foil-lined baking tray and bake in the oven for 10 minutes or until cooked through. Flake the fish off the skin, carefully removing any bones. Cut away the tough stalks from about 250g purple sprouting or ordinary broccoli. Put the broccoli in a steamer or a fine sieve balanced over a pan of boiling water. Cover and steam until tender, about 8 minutes. When the potato is cooked, cut it in half and scoop out the flesh, then mash it. Either purée the fish and broccoli together or chop them very finely on a board. Combine the fish and broccoli with the mashed potato, adding liquid as necessary. Makes about 300ml.

Pea & garlic

Bring a pan of water to the boil, drop in around 300g fresh or frozen peas (or petits pois) and 2 peeled whole garlic cloves. Return to a simmer. Cook until the peas are tender – around 5 minutes for frozen ones, probably longer for fresh. Drain, saving the water. Transfer the peas and garlic to a blender. Add about 50ml of the cooking water, and a knob of butter, if you like (provided your baby is over 6 months). Purée, adding a little more cooking water if necessary. Makes about 400ml.

Spinach, spelt & onion
Put 50g pearled spelt (or pearl barley) in a small pan and cover with
plenty of water. Bring to the boil and simmer briskly for about 20 minutes
until completely tender (barley will take longer). Drain, saving the water.
Wash 300g spinach and tear out tough stalks from mature leaves; baby
leaf spinach can be cooked whole. Put the spinach, with just the water
that clings to it from washing, into a saucepan. Place over a medium heat,
cover and let the spinach wilt in its own juices – this will only take 3–4
minutes. Tip into a colander to drain (but don't squeeze or press it). Finely
chop 1 small onion. Heat 1 tbsp rapeseed or olive oil in the spinach pan
over a medium heat. Add the onion and sauté gently for 10 minutes, to
soften. Combine the cooked spelt, spinach and onion in a blender and add
another 1 tbsp oil. Purée, adding a little of the reserved spelt cooking
water to help it along. Spelt gives the purée a lovely, nubbly texture.
Makes about 500ml.

Chicken & lettuce
Using strong kitchen scissors, cut 2 skinless, boneless chicken thighs into
even-sized chunks. Put them in a small pan and add enough water to just
cover. Bring to the boil, reduce the heat and simmer, stirring once or twice,
until the chicken is cooked right through, about 8 minutes. Meanwhile,
roughly chop 1 head of Cos (Romaine) lettuce. Add to the pan, stir, then
cover the pan. Cook for a further 3 minutes, stirring once or twice, or until
the lettuce has completely wilted. Transfer the whole lot to a blender and
purée. Makes about 300ml.

Beetroot, potato & Cheddar
Preheat the oven to 190°C/gas 5. Trim about 300g beetroot and scrub
well under cold running water. Scrub 2 small potatoes (about 200g). Put
the beetroot and potatoes in an ovenproof dish, cover with foil and bake
for around 1½ hours, or until a knife goes easily through them. As soon
as the potato is cool enough to handle, peel off the skin and mash the
flesh in a bowl. When the beetroot is cool enough to handle, peel away
the skins using a small knife. Chop the beetroot roughly, then purée in
a blender with about 50ml water. Combine the beetroot purée with the
mashed potato. Add 50g finely grated Cheddar (if your baby is over
6 months, otherwise leave out the cheese). Mix until evenly combined.
Makes about 500ml.

Squash & lentil

Peel, deseed and chop about 250g pumpkin or other squash. Put into a small saucepan with 50g red lentils and add enough water or freshly made, unsalted stock to just cover everything. Bring to a simmer. Cook, uncovered, for 20–30 minutes until both veg and lentils are soft, stirring frequently and mashing down the squash as you go. Add a little more water if needed, but keep the mixture quite thick. Mash completely with a fork, or purée. Makes about 400ml.

Variation: **Sweet potato & lentil**
This purée is also delicious made with sweet potato in place of squash.

Leek & celeriac

Trim and slice 2 large leeks. Peel and cube about 250g celeriac. Heat about 25g butter, or 2 tbsp rapeseed or olive oil, in a saucepan over a medium heat. Add the leeks and, as soon as they start to cook, turn the heat to low and put the lid on. Sweat them down gently, stirring from time to time, for about 10 minutes, or until really soft. Add the cubed celeriac and enough water or freshly made, unsalted stock to almost but not quite cover the veg. Bring to a simmer, cover and simmer for about 15 minutes, stirring once or twice, until all the celeriac is soft. Purée in a blender. Thin down individual portions with more stock or milk before serving if necessary. Makes about 400ml.

Leek, cabbage & potato

Trim and slice 1 large leek. Peel and cube 1 large potato (around 300g). Heat about 25g butter, or 2 tbsp rapeseed or olive oil, in a saucepan over a medium heat. Add the leek and, as soon as it starts to soften, turn the heat to low and put the lid on. Sweat gently, stirring occasionally, for about 10 minutes, until soft. Add the potato and enough water or freshly made, unsalted stock to just cover the veg. Bring to a simmer, cover and simmer for about 10 minutes, stirring once or twice, until the potato is almost done. Meanwhile, shred about ¼ green cabbage, such as Savoy, discarding any tough stalk. Add to the pan, with a little more water if needed, stir well and cook for another 5 minutes until the cabbage is tender. Purée in a blender, making sure the cabbage is reduced to very tiny pieces. Makes about 300ml.

Fruit-based purées

As soon as your baby is ready, make these purées more textured by
chopping or mashing the ingredients rather than liquidising them.
To make any of them more substantial, try the following:

- If your baby is over 6 months, add a dash of cream or some plain,
  full-fat yoghurt before serving.

- Add some freshly cooked pudding or risotto rice (not leftover rice,
  which can sometimes cause food poisoning).

- Combine the fruit purée with cooked porridge – made with oats or
  another grain (see page 117).

- You can also try adding a few new, spicy flavours – a pinch of ground
  cinnamon or a few drops of pure vanilla extract, for example.

Note: Citrus fruit and berries can occasionally cause an 'oral allergy
reaction' in some children (see page 76). Introduce them alongside other
fruits you know your child can eat so you can spot any reaction.

Apple, orange & banana

Peel, core and slice 2 medium dessert apples. Put in a steamer, or fine sieve
over a pan of simmering water. Cover and steam for about 10 minutes until
soft, stirring once or twice. Cool, then purée or mash with a banana and
enough freshly squeezed orange juice to get the consistency you want. As
this purée uses raw fruit, it's best eaten straight away. Makes about 150ml.

Apple & dried apricot

Put 100g dried apricots in a small pan, just cover them with water and
leave to soak overnight. Peel, core and slice 2 medium dessert apples and
add to the pan. Bring to a simmer and cook for about 10 minutes, stirring
often, until all the fruit is soft. Purée together. Makes about 300ml.

Pear & papaya

If you have a couple of nice, ripe, soft pears, you don't need to cook them:
simply peel and core the pears, then roughly chop the flesh. If the pears
are firm, peel, core and roughly chop, then put in a steamer or a fine
sieve balanced over a pan of simmering water, cover and steam for about

10 minutes, until soft. Leave to cool. Halve and deseed a papaya, scoop out the flesh and combine with the pear before puréeing. As this purée contains raw fruit, it's best to use it straight away. Makes about 300ml.

Rhubarb & apple

Preheat the oven to 170°C/gas 3. Wash 250g rhubarb and cut it into 3–4cm pieces. Place in an ovenproof dish with just the water clinging to it after washing. Peel, core and slice 4 medium dessert apples and add these too. Cover with foil and bake for about 25 minutes, until all the fruit is soft. Pour off the juice, then purée the fruit in a blender. The sweet apple should balance the tartness of the rhubarb nicely. However, if the rhubarb is particularly sharp, I would sweeten it with 1 tsp sifted icing sugar. Makes 300–400ml.

Mango & rice

Put 50g pudding or risotto rice in a small pan and cover with 200ml water. Bring to the boil, reduce the heat, cover and simmer very gently for about 20 minutes or until the rice is completely tender and all the water has been absorbed. Add a splash more water if needed. Cool the rice as quickly as possible, then put in a blender with the roughly chopped flesh of 1 large, ripe mango, and purée. As this uses raw fruit and rice, it should be served straight away. Add a squirt of lime juice and perhaps some chunks of fresh nectarine before serving to older family members. Makes about 350ml.

Berry & banana

Purée about 200g mixed berries – strawberries, blueberries, raspberries, blackberries etc. If you've used any with big pips, such as raspberries, push through a sieve to remove them. Combine the berry purée with 1 ripe banana, cut into chunks. Purée together. Because this purée uses raw fruit, it should be served straight away. Makes about 300ml.

Apple & raspberry or blackberry

Peel, core and slice 2–3 medium dessert apples. Put in a steamer or a fine sieve balanced over a pan of simmering water. Cover and steam for about 5 minutes, until soft. Cool. Meanwhile, purée about 250g raspberries, blackberries, or a mix of both, in a blender, then push through a sieve to remove the pips. Combine with the apple and purée together. Because this uses raw fruit, it should be served straight away. Makes about 300ml.

Purées as Family Food

It's not only babies who can enjoy purées, I'm sure you will relish some of these simple recipes yourself – just as they are (the fruit ones in particular), or use as the base for slightly more grown-up meals:

- Add butter and seasoning to a vegetable purée before serving as a side dish to meat or fish.

- Thin down a savoury purée with good chicken or vegetable stock and a dash of cream to make soup.

- Try a veg purée on toast. I like the pea and garlic one spooned, warm, onto toasted, garlic-rubbed sourdough bread and finished with a trickle of oil and some shavings of Parmesan.

- The fruit purées are great mixed with plain, full-fat yoghurt to make delicious, home-made alternatives to shop-bought fruit yoghurts.

- Try fruit purée spooned onto porridge or even toast in place of jam.

- Serve fruit purées with ice cream or rice pudding, or use as the base of a smoothie.

SPRING
(March, April, May)

Porridge

Classic oat porridge is hard to beat – filling and sustaining, relatively rich in protein (for a cereal) and a decent source of iron too. However, alternative grains can be used for a hot breakfast and are particularly useful if you're avoiding gluten (oats contain a protein very similar to gluten). Millet is rich in B vitamins and makes a mild, sweetish porridge that's very nice with fruit. Quinoa (pronounced 'keen-wa') is something of a supergrain, being rich in protein and other nutrients, including iron. It's a very good choice for vegetarians as the protein it contains is 'complete' (it has all the amino acids the body needs). Both millet flakes and quinoa flakes are available from healthfood shops and some supermarkets.

For babies: Do not give sultanas to very young babies as they could be a choking risk.

PUT the oats, millet or quinoa in a small pan with the milk and/or water. Bring to the boil, stirring often to break up any lumps, then reduce the heat to low. Simmer, stirring frequently, for about 3 minutes, until the mixture is thick and the grains tender. Be careful as the thickening porridge can spit while it cooks.

Cool the porridge a little before serving. You can thin and cool it with a splash of cold milk, or stir in some fruit purée. In fact, any fresh, dried or stewed fruit is a good accompaniment (see variation below). A trickle of honey is lovely too, for anyone over 12 months.

Variation
Apple and sultana porridge This works well with any of the above grains, and is a nice way to sweeten porridge without adding refined sugar. Just add 1 heaped tbsp sultanas to the oats, millet or quinoa before you start cooking them. Then, when the porridge is cooked, stir in 2–3 tbsp apple purée (see page 105).

2 adult servings

100g porridge oats (not jumbo), millet flakes or quinoa flakes

500ml whole milk or water, or a blend of both

Mango smoothie

The 'hungry gap' period of spring, when there are few homegrown fruits around, is a good time to make use of imported treats such as mangoes and oranges. You could substitute apple juice for the orange, but the orange and mango combination gives a particularly delicious, almost sherbet-like flavour. In the summer, you can also make this breakfast smoothie using very ripe peaches instead of the mango. If your family prefers their smoothies super-chilled, refrigerate the fruit beforehand.

For babies: This is a nice thick smoothie that could be put on a spoon or dunked with a bit of plain toast.

SLICE the mango either side of the stone, then slice out the flesh from inside the skin. Cut the remaining flesh off the mango, trimming away the skin as you go. If you discover a way of doing this without getting yourself all sticky and dripping with juice, do let me know.

Put the mango flesh in a blender with the yoghurt and orange juice. Blitz until smooth, then serve.

Per adult serving

1 ripe mango

2–3 tbsp plain, full-fat yoghurt

Juice of 1 orange

Cauliflower soup

Homegrown caulis are available most of the year and they're a great mainstay during the spring when not much other British veg is available. Full of antioxidants, they make a lovely, creamy soup that can be augmented with all sorts of tasty toppings – a few crunchy croûtons and some grated cheese always go down well in our house, or you could simply serve cheese on toast fingers alongside for dipping.

FREEZER FRIENDLY

For babies: This is quite a thick soup so it can function as a purée too.

For grown-ups and older children: Top with crumbled blue cheese, some feisty chilli oil, or shards of fried bacon.

HEAT the butter or oil in a large saucepan over a medium heat. Add the onion, garlic, celery and potato, reduce the heat, cover the pan and sweat gently for 5–10 minutes, until all the veg are softened.

Add the cauliflower, the stock (which should only barely cover the veg) and the bay leaf. Bring to the boil, reduce the heat, cover and simmer gently for about 15 minutes or until the cauliflower and potato are completely tender.

Remove the bay leaf, then purée the soup until smooth. Add some seasoning if you like, and serve.

6 adult servings

25g butter or 2 tbsp rapeseed or olive oil

1 onion, roughly chopped

1 garlic clove, roughly chopped

1 celery stalk, sliced

1 medium potato (about 220g), peeled and cubed

1 large cauliflower (about 1kg), trimmed and roughly chopped

About 750ml chicken or vegetable stock (see pages 236–8)

1 bay leaf

Freshly ground black pepper and salt (optional)

Champ-cannon

Champ is a comforting Irish dish of mashed potato and spring onions. Colcannon, also from Ireland, is a tasty dish of mashed potato and shredded greens. I find that combining the two – into a buttery mound of vegetably goodness – works brilliantly.

For babies: Chop the cabbage and spring onions, rather than simply shred them, to make the dish easier to eat. To make this a more complete meal, stir some finely chopped hard-boiled egg or grated cheese into the mash.

For grown-ups and older children: Champ-cannon is wonderful with a freshly poached egg broken on top.

PEEL the potatoes, cut into even-sized chunks and put in a saucepan. Cover with cold water, bring to the boil, then reduce the heat. Put the lid on and simmer for 15–20 minutes or until completely tender.

Meanwhile, bring another pan of water to the boil and drop in the shredded cabbage. Let it simmer for 3–4 minutes, until tender, then drain well.

Put the spring onions, milk and butter in a small pan. Bring up to a simmer and cook gently, stirring often, for a few minutes, until the onions are soft. Combine with the drained cabbage and stir together well.

Drain the potatoes well and leave them to steam for a few minutes in the colander. Return to their still-hot pan and mash them – or rice them back into the pan. Add the onion and cabbage mixture, and some seasoning if you like. Mix well, and serve.

Try with sausages, goujons (see page 137) or baked and flaked fish (see page 239).

3 adult servings, as a side dish

750g floury potatoes, such as Maris Piper, King Edward or Wilja

½ head of Savoy or other green cabbage, or 1 head of spring greens, tough stalks removed, finely shredded

2 bunches of spring onions, trimmed and finely sliced

75ml whole milk

30g unsalted butter

Freshly ground black pepper and sea salt (optional)

PSB Pasta

Purple sprouting broccoli is a seasonal treat, available from March to early May. The slender stems are delicious lightly cooked on their own (and very good finger food), but also excellent with pasta. This recipe works well with standard broccoli (calabrese) too.

For babies: Go easy on the chilli or leave it out. As with many dishes, this works best for babies if you either keep the pieces really small and spoonable (use tiny pasta shapes and chop the broccoli finely), or if you keep them big and grabbable.

PUT a large pan of water on to boil. When it comes to the boil, add the pasta shapes. Cook for the time recommended on the packet (probably 10–12 minutes), giving it a good stir from time to time.

Meanwhile, heat the oil in a frying pan over a medium heat. Add the onion and garlic, and chilli if using, and reduce the heat a little. Sweat them gently, stirring often, for about 10 minutes until soft but not browned.

Trim the broccoli (the stems can be woody at the ends). Cut the tops into small florets and the tender stems into small pieces. Make sure you keep the lovely, tender little leaves on the stem too. When the pasta is about 5 minutes off the end of its cooking time, add the broccoli to it.

Once the pasta and broccoli are cooked, drain well. Add the fried onion, garlic and chilli mixture and toss together well. Season if you like, then serve, with grated cheese.

3 adult servings

250g pasta shapes of your choice

3 tbsp rapeseed or olive oil

1 onion, chopped

1 garlic clove, chopped

½ red chilli, deseeded and finely chopped (optional)

About 250g purple sprouting broccoli

Freshly ground black pepper and sea salt (optional)

Freshly grated Parmesan or other hard cheese, to serve

Avocado & houmous salad

Avocado is definitely an important part of my child-friendly repertoire. It's nutritious, versatile and easy to prepare – an instant portable meal, in fact, as you can spoon it straight from the skin if you want to.

This substantial salad is one of my favourite quick lunches. I sometimes embellish my portion with a few chunks of really good, char-grilled, oil-preserved artichoke heart. These are a treat though, as they're expensive, and too salty for babies.

For babies: Keep the avocado in big, long pieces to make them easy to grab. Or mash the avocado with the houmous for spooning or spreading.

For grown-ups and older children: A few toasted walnuts are a delicious and nutritious finishing touch.

ARRANGE the salad leaves in deep serving dishes. Halve the avocado, remove the stone, and peel off the skin. Cut the flesh into bite-sized pieces, or long slices, whatever you prefer, and arrange over the leaves.

Add a few little dollops of houmous to each plate, in between the avocado pieces, then trickle over a little oil.

Finish each dish with a few shavings of cheese – and a good grinding of black pepper if you like. Serve straight away (the avocado will start to brown after a while).

3 adult servings

A couple of handfuls of lettuce or other salad leaves
1 large avocado
A few good dollops of houmous (shop-bought or home-made, see page 245)
A little extra virgin rapeseed or olive oil
A little Parmesan or other well-flavoured hard cheese
Freshly ground black pepper

Frittata

You can customise this recipe to your heart's content. Almost any cooked vegetable can go in, from spring broccoli through summer peas, beans and courgettes to winter roots, and it can be enhanced with chopped herbs.

For babies: Wedges or chunks of frittata are good finger food.

For grown-ups and older children: This is ideal picnic or lunchbox fare.

IF COOKING potatoes from scratch, scrub or scrape them clean and cut into chunky cubes. Put in a pan, cover with water, bring to the boil, then lower the heat and simmer for about 10 minutes until tender. If using cooked potatoes, cut into cubes. Meanwhile, snap off the woody ends of the asparagus, wash the spears, then cut into roughly 3cm pieces. Add to the potato pan for the last 3–4 minutes. Drain the veg well.

Lightly beat the eggs together and season them if you like. Preheat your grill to medium-high.

Heat the oil in a 25–28cm non-stick frying pan over a medium heat. Add the spring onions and fry gently for about 5 minutes, until soft and wilted. Add the potato cubes and asparagus and stir with the onions. Make sure the ingredients are distributed evenly around the pan.

Now pour in the beaten eggs. Don't move the egg around, just keep the pan over a medium heat and let it set slowly. After around 5 minutes, the base of the frittata will be set but the top will still be wet.

Sprinkle the cheese over the top, then put the frittata under the grill for 3–5 minutes, until cooked through and golden brown on top. Let cool for at least 10 minutes before slicing (in the pan or out) and serving. Best warm or cold, not hot.

4–6 adult servings

350g new potatoes (leftover cooked ones are ideal)
1 bunch of asparagus (about 300g, or 15 stems)
7 medium eggs
2 tbsp rapeseed or olive oil
2 bunches of spring onions, trimmed and sliced
75g Cheddar or other well-flavoured hard cheese
Freshly ground black pepper and sea salt (optional)

Saag paneer

Paneer is a very mild Indian cheese, usually made without salt. It's a satisfying addition to salads, stir-fries, pasta sauces etc, but I particularly love it in this mildly spiced dish. Paneer is sold in most supermarkets and many healthfood shops but, if you can't find it, try tofu instead. You could use tender chard leaves instead of spinach (remove and chop the stalks to use in a stir-fry or pasta dish). The tender first nettle tops of spring would work very well in this too (for nettle preparation, see page 29).

For babies: Go easy on the chilli, or leave it out. Your baby will need reasonably good chewing skills to tackle chunks of paneer, or you can chop the whole dish finely to make it spoonable.

I F THE spinach is quite mature and has some tough stalks, tear them out and discard. Wash the spinach thoroughly then pack it, with just the water that clings to it, into a saucepan. Cover, put over a medium heat and cook until the spinach has wilted in its own liquid – just a few minutes. Drain and leave in the colander to cool. When cool enough to handle, squeeze out as much liquid as you can with your hands, then chop the spinach roughly.

Heat the oil in a frying pan and gently sweat the onion for 5–10 minutes, until soft. Add the garlic, chilli if using, ginger, garam masala and cubed paneer. Cook for another couple of minutes, then add the chopped spinach and cream. Cook briefly to warm through, season if you like, and serve.

Try serving with pitta bread (for home-made, see pages 229–31) or chapatis or, for a more substantial dish, with lamb curry (see page 165) and rice.

3–4 adult servings, with accompaniments

400g spinach
2 tbsp rapeseed or sunflower oil
1 onion, thinly sliced
1 garlic clove, finely chopped
½ red chilli, deseeded and finely chopped (optional)
1 good tsp grated fresh ginger
2 tsp garam masala
200g paneer, cut into cubes
4–6 tbsp double cream
Freshly ground black pepper and sea salt (optional)

Lentils with onion & watercress

This is a soft, soothing little dish of cooked lentils, perked up with peppery watercress and sweetened with fried onions. It's easy-to-eat comfort food, but also very nutritious – packed with protein and a good source of iron, vitamin C and antioxidants. Serve with rice to create a vegetarian meal with complete protein. It's also a nice accompaniment to chicken or baked fish or any kind of curry.

FREEZER FRIENDLY

For babies: This can function as a purée, or your baby can dip into it with a chunk of rice cake, or some vegetable batons.

PUT the lentils and chopped garlic in a saucepan with 400ml water. Bring to the boil, turn down to a gentle simmer and cook, stirring often, for about 20 minutes, until the mixture is thick and the lentils are starting to break down, adding a little more water if necessary.

Meanwhile, bring a pan of water to the boil, drop in the watercress and cook for a minute or so, just until it's completely wilted. Drain and leave to cool in a colander. When it's cool enough to handle, squeeze out all the water, then chop fairly finely.

Heat the oil in a frying pan over a medium heat. Add the onion and fry for about 10 minutes, stirring often and keeping the heat at medium. The idea is to get the onion to start to caramelise and brown just a little.

Combine the cooked lentils with the chopped watercress and cooked onion. Season if you like, and serve hot with rice or bread.

3–4 adult servings, with accompaniments

100g red lentils

1 garlic clove, finely chopped

200–250g watercress, tough stems removed

2 tbsp rapeseed or olive oil

1 onion, finely chopped

Freshly ground black pepper and sea salt (optional)

Fishcakes

These are good served with petits pois. They include cornichons, which are quite salty, so don't add extra salt. The uncooked fishcakes freeze well.

FREEZER FRIENDLY

For babies: *Leave out the cornichons.*

PREHEAT the oven to 200°C/gas 6. Bake the potatoes for 1–1½ hours, until tender. Cut in half, scrape out the flesh and either mash or rice it into a large bowl. Let cool.

Meanwhile, brush the fish fillets with oil and lay skin-side down in a foil-lined ovenproof dish. Bake for 10 minutes or until cooked through. Leave to cool, then break into flakes, discarding the skin and any bones. Add to the potato.

Heat 1–2 tbsp oil in a small frying pan over a medium heat. Add the onion and fry gently for 10 minutes until soft and golden. Add to the fish and potato, with the cornichons and parsley, and a little lemon zest and pepper, if you like.

Take heaped dessertspoonfuls of the mixture, roll into balls and then squash gently to form cakes, no more than 2.5cm thick. Dip each fishcake in flour, then dust off the excess. Dip in beaten egg and let the excess drain off, then coat with breadcrumbs, patting them on lightly. (You can also cook the fishcakes with just the flour coating.)

To cook, heat a thin layer of oil (about 1mm) in a non-stick frying pan over a medium heat. Add the fishcakes and fry for about 3 minutes until the base is golden brown and crusted. Carefully flip them over and cook for another 3 minutes or so, or until golden brown and piping hot in the middle (they may need longer if they've been in the fridge). Serve with peas, or cucumber sticks.

Makes about 10

2 large baking potatoes
About 400g fish fillets – try pollack, sustainably caught haddock or cod, gurnard, salmon or mackerel (see page 23)
Rapeseed or olive oil, for brushing and frying
1 small onion, finely chopped
2–3 cornichons, or 1 small gherkin, finely chopped
1 tbsp chopped parsley
A little finely grated lemon zest (optional)
Freshly ground black pepper (optional)

To finish
2 tbsp plain flour
1 large egg, beaten
75g breadcrumbs

Salmon risotto

Risotto is such a versatile dish and this one can be tinkered with a fair bit, if the fancy takes you. Replace the spring onion with standard onion, or the white part of a leek. If purple sprouting broccoli is not to hand, add some ordinary broccoli. You could also use other fish – or even shellfish (see variations). When it comes to the stock, as ever, home-made is best – veg stock works really well but if you make your own fish stock at home, use that instead. A light chicken stock can stand in too.

For babies: This is a lovely way to serve fish to babies. You can chop or mash the finished risotto if you like.

For grown-ups and older children: A dollop of pesto or a sprinkling of gremolata (finely chopped garlic, parsley and lemon zest) is a nice, peppy finishing touch. You could also add about 50ml white wine to the rice before you start adding the stock.

HEAT the oil in a fairly large saucepan over a medium heat. Add the spring onions and sweat them gently for about 5 minutes, until soft. Meanwhile, bring the stock to a low simmer in a separate small pan, then turn the heat right down to keep the stock hot.

Add the rice to the onions and stir for a minute or two. Now start adding the hot stock, a ladleful at a time. Stir frequently and add a fresh ladleful of hot stock only once the previous one has been absorbed by the rice.

As the rice is cooking, slice the salmon off the skin, carefully remove any bones, then cut the fish into small cubes.

After you've been cooking and stirring the risotto for about 15 minutes, add the broccoli tips. Keep cooking, adding the stock bit by bit and stirring frequently, until you have added all or most of the stock and the rice is cooked and tender – probably a further 8 minutes.

3 adult servings

2 tbsp rapeseed or olive oil
1 large bunch of spring onions, finely sliced
About 1 litre vegetable stock (see page 238) or fish stock
250g risotto rice
250g salmon fillet (see page 23)
A handful of purple sprouting broccoli tips, chopped into small pieces
A knob of unsalted butter (about 10g)
A squeeze of lemon juice
Freshly ground black pepper and sea salt (optional)

Stir in the salmon and cook, stirring occasionally, for 2–3 minutes, until the fish is done. Turn off the heat, and dot the butter over the top. Cover the pan for a minute or two so the butter melts, then stir the butter into the rice. Add a squeeze of lemon juice, season if you like, and serve straight away.

Variations

For a nice, economical way to introduce a child to the flavour of shellfish, replace 50–100g of the salmon with a few scallops or mussels, as follows:

Risotto with scallops Use 6–8 diver-caught scallops, cleaned and trimmed. I use just the white muscle, not the coral. Slice the scallops horizontally in half. Put a trickle of oil in a frying pan over a high heat. When hot, add the scallops and fry for about 2 minutes, or until they have formed a crust and can be easily moved in the pan. Flip them over and cook for another 1 minute. Chop, if you like, before adding to the risotto with the salmon.

Risotto with mussels Use 400–500g rope-grown mussels. Scrub under cold running water, using a small sharp knife to remove any barnacles and wiry 'beards'. Discard any mussels with broken or damaged shells, and any that are open and do not close when tapped sharply against the side of the sink. Put the mussels in a large pan (they should be only one mussel deep) with a ladleful of the hot stock that you're using in the risotto. Cover with a tight-fitting lid and put over a high heat. Let the mussels steam for 3–4 minutes, or until they are all clearly open. If there are any which do not open, discard them. Pinch the mussels out of their shells and add, whole or chopped, to the risotto with the salmon.

Advice on giving shellfish to babies and toddlers

Parents are advised not to give shellfish – or any fish, for that matter – to a baby under 6 months. This is partly because of the small risk of food poisoning (which could be serious for a young baby), and partly because it's not yet clear whether very early introduction of fish may constitute an allergy risk. Over 6 months, you can start to introduce shellfish carefully, always on the proviso that it is from a reliable source, very fresh and well cooked. Offer it in small amounts, either on its own, or with foods you know your child can eat, so you can note any adverse reaction. Shellfish sold in the UK is subject to rigorous testing to ensure that it's safe to eat. Thorough cooking should destroy any lingering bacteria and viruses.

A simple chowder

Chowders are milk-based soups, usually containing fish and potatoes – nutritious and tasty stuff. I've made this one pretty thick so that it's easy for a small person to get on their spoon. You can always add a little more milk if you prefer something more liquid.

For babies: Leave out the smoked fish, as it's a little salty (you can set a baby portion aside before adding the smoked fish right at the end of cooking). Chop the prawns if you need to. If your baby has never eaten prawns or fish before, you should introduce them one at a time, not together, just in case there's any kind of reaction.

HEAT the butter in a saucepan over a medium heat. When it's melted, add the leek and sweat down gently for 5–10 minutes, until soft. Stir in the potato, then the milk. Bring to a simmer, cover, and simmer gently for about 15 minutes, stirring often, until the potato is tender.

Meanwhile, slice the white fish and smoked fish off their skin. Carefully remove any bones, then cut the fish into small pieces.

When the potatoes are cooked, stir the fish and the prawns into the chowder. Continue to cook very gently, stirring often, for 3–4 minutes, or until the fish is cooked through. Add the herbs if you're using them, season if you like, then serve straight away.

3 adult servings

A large knob of butter

1 leek, trimmed, quartered lengthways and finely sliced

1 medium potato (about 220g), peeled and cut into small cubes

350ml whole milk

200g white fish, such as pollack, or sustainably caught haddock or cod (see page 23)

75g smoked pollack or haddock

100g cooked, shelled cold-water prawns

1 tbsp chopped parsley and/or chives (optional)

Freshly ground black pepper and sea salt (optional)

Golden goujons

If you make these with chicken, I recommend buying thigh meat rather than breast, as it's more succulent, and cheaper. Or you can try any other poultry. This recipe can be used to make delicious, free-form fish fingers, too – it's a particularly nice way to introduce children to mackerel.

FREEZER FRIENDLY *Prepare the goujons then freeze uncooked. Defrost in the fridge before frying.*

For babies: *These are great finger food.*

For grown-ups and older children: *You can pep up the coating by adding cayenne pepper or smoked paprika and lots of black pepper to the flour.*

CUT the meat or fish into easy-grab fingers or chunks, not too thick. Put the flour on a plate and season it, if you like. Put the eggs in a second shallow dish. Put the breadcrumbs on a third plate and mix in the thyme, if using.

Take a piece of meat or fish, dust it lightly in the flour, shaking off any excess, dip in beaten egg, allowing the excess to drip off, then coat in breadcrumbs, pressing them on lightly with your fingers. Put on a plate. Repeat until all the pieces are coated.

Pour a 1–2mm layer of oil into a non-stick frying pan and place over a medium heat. When the oil is hot, add the pieces to the pan (you'll probably have to cook them in two batches). Fry for 3–4 minutes each side (only about 2 minutes per side for fish), or until the goujons are golden, crisp and piping hot in the middle. Drain on kitchen paper.

Serve alongside something to dip them in: tomato sauce, mayonnaise, tartare sauce, garlicky yoghurt etc, and salady things such as cucumber, tomatoes and celery.

Makes about 20

250g boned-out chicken, or other poultry; or firm-fleshed fish, such as pollack or mackerel, skinned and deboned

3 tbsp plain flour

2 eggs, lightly beaten

100g fine, slightly dry breadcrumbs (brown or white)

1 tsp finely chopped thyme (optional)

Rapeseed, olive or sunflower oil, for frying

Freshly ground black pepper and sea salt (optional)

Roast chicken

There are lots of things you can add to a roasting chicken to bring a bit of variety (herbs, lemon, wine, spices etc) but, if you've got a good bird to start with, you can keep it simple. Roast your chicken on a Sunday and you've got dinner for two grown-ups and two children, leftover cold meat for a couple of lunches, and a carcass that will yield wonderful, flavoursome stock (see page 237). It goes without saying that I prefer a free-range or organic bird...

For babies: When the chicken is cooked, select a little of the moist thigh meat. If you're doing baby-led weaning, give this just as it is, in long pieces. Alternatively, combine the meat with some of the gravy and whatever veg you're having and chop finely or purée. One of the yummiest baby dinners ever...

TAKE the chicken out of the fridge about an hour before cooking so it comes up to room temperature. Preheat the oven to 210°C/gas 7.

Untruss the chicken and put it in a smallish roasting dish. If it has a bag of giblets inside, remove them. Separate out the liver (you can freeze chicken livers and, when you've got a few, use them to make pâté, see page 141). Put the remaining giblets in the fridge ready for stock-making.

Pull the chicken's legs away from its body slightly, so hot air can circulate. Brush the oil all over the bird – or smear with the soft butter. Season the skin with salt and pepper. You can leave out this seasoning, but it's a shame to do so as it creates such delicious skin – just don't give the skin to a baby under 12 months (it would be hard for them to chew in any case).

Scatter the chopped onion and celery around the chicken and tuck the bay inside it. Put into the oven and roast for 20 minutes.

(continued overleaf)

3 adult servings, with plenty of leftovers

1 medium chicken (1.75–2kg)
2–3 tbsp rapeseed or olive oil, or soft, unsalted butter
1 onion, roughly chopped
1 celery stalk, roughly chopped
1–2 bay leaves
2 tsp plain flour (optional)
Freshly ground black pepper and sea salt (optional)

Take the chicken from the oven and pour a glass of water into the roasting tin (not over the bird). Lower the oven setting to 180°C/gas 4, return the chicken to the oven and cook for a further 40 minutes.

Now turn the oven off, prop the door open slightly and leave the chicken inside for a further 15 minutes to finish cooking. Check that the bird is cooked by plunging a skewer deep into the thickest part of the meat, where the leg joins the body. Press with a spoon – the juices that run out should be clear with no trace of blood in them. If they are at all pink, the chicken is not cooked, so return it to the oven, switch back on to 180°C/gas 4 and cook for a further 10 minutes, then test again.

Tip up the chicken to allow any juices inside to run out into the roasting dish. Transfer the chicken to a warmed plate and, if possible, get someone else to carve the meat while you make a simple gravy. Strain the juices into a jug. Discard the bay leaf and set the veg aside, keeping them warm.

Put the roasting tin over a medium heat. Add 2–3 tsp of the fat spooned from the surface of the juices (skim off and discard the rest of the fat). Scatter the flour into the roasting tin, if using, and stir it into the fat (flour helps to emulsify the little bit of fat). Now add a slosh of the hot juices from the jug and stir into the floury paste. Repeat once or twice until all the juices are back in the tin and bubbling away. Keep simmering briskly, stirring often, to reduce and intensify the gravy. Stop when it tastes good to you. You can season it further now if you like.

Serve the hot chicken with the hot gravy, reserved celery and onion, and any other veg you fancy. Potatoes – boiled, mashed or roast – are always popular. Couscous is also good with roast chicken, as it soaks up the savoury juices nicely.

Leftover chicken should be left to cool, then refrigerated for sandwiches, salads or snacks over the next few days. Don't throw away the chicken carcass – use it to make stock (see page 237).

Chicken liver pâté

Liver is a very rich source of vitamin A – so rich, in fact, that you shouldn't give it to your child more than once a week in case they get too much. But an occasional serving of this very tasty pâté is a good way to provide protein and iron. I'm very grateful to paediatric dietitian Judy More, whose original recipe this is based on.

For babies: Offer a thin scraping of this on toast.

TRIM the chicken livers, removing any discoloured or greenish parts. Put the livers in a small bowl and add enough milk to just cover them. Leave to soak for about 2 hours, then drain (this helps to remove any bitterness). Discard the milk. Chop the livers roughly.

Heat the butter in a wide frying pan over a medium heat. Add the onion or shallot, celery and garlic and cook gently for about 5 minutes, until soft. Add the livers and the thyme. Sauté for 10–15 minutes, until the livers are cooked through and nicely browned.

You can now just mash everything together with a fork to get a nice, coarse-textured pâté. Alternatively, blend in a food processor to get a smooth result. Either way, season if you like, then leave to cool.

Serve the pâté spread on toast with some crunchy raw veg, such as carrot or celery, or tomato, on the side.

3–4 adult servings, as a starter or light meal

200g chicken livers

Milk, for soaking

50g unsalted butter

½ small onion, or 1 large shallot, finely chopped

1 celery stalk, finely chopped

1 garlic clove, finely chopped

1–2 tsp chopped thyme

Freshly ground black pepper and sea salt (optional)

Oaty rhubarb crumble

This crumble topping uses oats and fine oatmeal, so it's wheat-free. You can use it on top of other fruits – try peeled, cored and sliced apple, tossed with sugar, sultanas and cinnamon (or blackberries, see page 26), or stoned and quartered plums, trickled with a little maple syrup.

FREEZER FRIENDLY *Make up a double or triple quantity of the topping mixture and freeze the excess for use later on.*

For babies: You can mash the crumble – perhaps loosening with a little cream – to make it easier for a younger baby to eat from a spoon.

REHEAT the oven to 180°C/gas 4.

To make the crumble topping, put the oatmeal, oats and butter in a food processor and pulse briefly until the butter is worked into the oatmeal and the mixture resembles fine crumbs – don't overdo it, or it will start to clump together too much. Tip into a bowl and stir in the demerara sugar.

Wash the rhubarb and cut it into 1–2cm pieces. Spread it in an ovenproof dish (about a 2 litre capacity). Squeeze the orange juice over it, or sprinkle on the apple juice, then evenly scatter over the caster sugar. This amount of sugar should be fine for new season, forced rhubarb – the slender-stemmed, bright pink stuff. If you're using robust, outdoor-grown rhubarb later in the year, you might need a little more.

Spoon the oaty topping over the rhubarb in an even layer. Bake for about 45 minutes until golden brown on top and bubbling underneath. Serve hot, warm or cold with cream, yoghurt or custard.

6 adult servings

For the crumble topping
125g fine oatmeal
125g porridge oats (not jumbo)
100g cold, unsalted butter, cut into small cubes
65g demerara sugar

For the fruit
750g rhubarb, trimmed
Juice of 1 orange, or about 75ml apple juice
50g caster sugar

Orange jelly

A wibbly wobbly way to get some vitamin C in the winter months, this jelly can, of course, be served at any time of year. In the summer, it's lovely if you replace some of the orange juice with puréed, sieved raspberries.

For babies: There's a reasonable amount of sugar in this, though most of it comes from the fruit juice, so I probably wouldn't offer it to a young baby.

SQUEEZE the juice from the oranges and pass through a sieve to remove the fibres and pips. You need 500ml juice, so keep squeezing until you have enough. Whisk enough icing sugar into the juice to sweeten it to your taste – I find 25g usually about right.

Soak the gelatine leaves in a bowl of cold water for about 10 minutes, until soft. Meanwhile, put 100ml of the orange juice into a small pan. Remove the soaked gelatine from the water, squeeze out excess water, then add to the orange juice in the pan. Heat very gently, stirring, for a minute or two until the gelatine has fully dissolved. Don't let it boil.

Combine the gelatined juice with the remaining orange juice and mix well.

You can use a jelly mould or pudding basin, or several small moulds, ramekins or cups. If you want to turn the jelly out, very lightly grease your mould first with a few drops of oil.

Pour the jelly into the mould(s). Chill until set, which should take 3–4 hours.

To unmould the jellies, fill a large bowl with very hot water. Dip the mould into it for a few seconds, then remove. Put an upturned plate over the top, then invert both plate and mould: the jelly should plop out. If it doesn't, repeat. Serve alone, or with fresh fruit (or, of course, with ice cream).

4 adult servings

About 5 large oranges or 8 medium ones

About 25g icing sugar

About 6–8 sheets leaf gelatine (brands vary in their setting capacity – from the packet instructions, calculate the number you need to set 500ml liquid)

A few drops of sunflower oil (optional)

SUMMER
(June, July, August)

Blueberry pancakes

These fruit-studded drop scones are a great way to start the day. If your children object to cooked blueberries, make the pancake batter without them and serve the berries raw on the side.

For babies: Cut the pancakes into grabbable strips and leave off the honey or syrup.

PUT the flours, baking powder and sugar in a large bowl and combine thoroughly. Lightly beat the eggs together with the milk, then pour slowly into the flour, whisking all the time, to form a smooth batter. Stir in the melted butter, then the blueberries.

Heat a little oil in a large, non-stick frying pan over a medium heat. Drop small ladlefuls of the batter into the pan, cook for a couple of minutes, until bubbles start to appear on the surface of the pancakes, then flip over and cook for a couple of minutes more. Check that the first one or two are cooked right through to the middle, so you know you're getting the timing right. Remove to a warmed plate, and repeat with the remaining batter, adding a little more oil to the pan if necessary.

Serve the pancakes warm, with a smear of butter and a trickle of honey (not for under-ones) or maple syrup.

Makes about 20

125g self-raising flour
125g wholemeal self-raising flour (or just use 250g white self-raising if you prefer)
½ level tsp baking powder
25g caster sugar
2 medium eggs, lightly beaten
275ml whole milk
50g unsalted butter, melted
150–200g blueberries
Sunflower oil, for cooking

To serve
A little unsalted butter
A little honey or maple syrup

Mini muesli with banana & strawberries

This is just a very simple kind of uncooked porridge. You can make up a batch of the muesli mix and keep it in an airtight tub, ready for breakfast time. The quinoa flakes and wheatgerm (both available from healthfood shops) are very nutritious additions, but you can vary the grains – try millet flakes, for instance. And of course, different chopped fruits can stand in for the strawberries.

For babies: Use fine porridge oats – young babies may prefer theirs chopped, as I suggest here. But you can dispense with this step when they're a little older.

For grown-ups and older children: You can add chunky 'jumbo' oats, for more texture, as well as whole or chopped nuts and seeds.

PUT the oats in a food processor and whiz until finely chopped, then combine with the quinoa flakes and wheatgerm. Store in an airtight container. Because the mix contains wheatgerm, which has a high oil content and can turn rancid, it's best kept in the fridge and used within a few weeks.

For a small serving, put 2 tbsp of the muesli mix in a small bowl and add about 3 tbsp milk (you can use breast or formula milk for a baby). Stir well and leave for about 10 minutes to soften. Meanwhile, chop the strawberry (finely, if this is for a younger baby). Mash the banana and stir into the muesli, then fold in the strawberry and serve.

About 10 small servings

100g porridge oats
50g quinoa flakes
25g toasted wheatgerm

Per serving
A little milk
1–2 large strawberries
A little banana – a 3cm piece for a baby

Spinach & onion puff tart

This is lovely on its own as a light meal, but it's also good alongside pulses, such as simply cooked red lentils (see page 129) or even baked beans. The spinach and onion mix can also be used as a base for baked eggs, or in frittatas or quiches, or in Helen's egg parcels (see page 180).

For babies: Try offering pieces of this as finger food.

For grown-ups and older children: The spinach mix is a lovely topping for bruschetta. Toast slices of sourdough, rub with garlic and trickle with olive oil, then pile the spinach mix on top and finish with crumbled goat's cheese or shavings of Parmesan.

PREHEAT the oven to 190°C/gas 5. Grease a baking tray or line with a non-stick liner.

If the spinach is mature, tear out any tough stalks. Wash the spinach thoroughly, then pack it, with just the water that clings to it, into a saucepan. Cover, put over a medium heat and wilt the spinach in its own liquid – this takes only a few minutes. Drain and leave in a colander to cool. When cool enough to handle, squeeze out as much liquid as you can with your hands, then chop the spinach roughly.

Meanwhile, heat the oil in a frying pan over a medium heat. Add the onion and cook gently, stirring often, for 10–15 minutes, until really soft and golden. Add the garlic for the last few minutes. Add the thyme leaves, then the chopped spinach, and season if you like.

Roll out the puff pastry on a lightly floured surface to a square, about 5mm thick, and lift onto the baking tray. Spread the spinach mix over the pastry, leaving a margin along the edges. Scatter over the grated cheese and bake for 15–20 minutes or until the pastry is puffed and golden, and the cheese is turning golden too. Serve warm or cold.

4 adult servings

350–400g spinach
2 tbsp rapeseed or olive oil
1 onion, quartered and finely chopped
1 garlic clove, cut into slivers
1 tsp chopped thyme leaves
375g good-quality ready-made all-butter puff pastry (ready-rolled is useful)
50g Cheddar or other hard cheese, grated
Freshly ground black pepper and sea salt (optional)

Three dips for dunking

You can dip anything you like into these thick, rich and flavourful dips, but I like to use them to encourage the whole family to enjoy lots of raw, crunchy veg. So offer them with crudités such as celery, carrot, cucumber and pepper strips, raw broccoli or cauliflower florets and lettuce leaves.

For babies: Hard, raw vegetables such as carrot can be a choking risk for small babies, so offer them softer crudités such as cucumber – or try lightly cooked and cooled sticks of carrot.

Courgette & cheese dip

This thick, green-flecked purée is a favourite of mine and very good for a summer lunch.

For grown-ups and older children: This is nice on brown toast or oatcakes topped with curls of smoked mackerel or salmon.

SLICE the courgettes thinly. Heat the butter and oil in a frying pan over a medium heat. Add the courgettes and garlic and fry gently, stirring often, until the courgettes are completely soft and translucent – this can take as long as 15–20 minutes. Leave to cool.

Transfer the courgettes to a food processor. Add the cream cheese, a squeeze of lemon juice, a little black pepper and a pinch of salt if you like (remember that the cheese also provides salt). Blitz the mixture to a thick purée.

Refrigerate the dip until needed, but bring up to cool room temperature before serving.

3 adult servings

About 250g courgettes

A knob of unsalted butter

A dash of rapeseed or olive oil

1 small garlic clove, chopped

50g cream cheese or soft, mild goat's cheese

A squeeze of lemon juice

Freshly ground black pepper and sea salt (optional)

Tangy tofu dip

It's important to use smooth, 'silken' tofu here – available in healthfood shops and many supermarkets – rather than standard tofu. What you end up with is a very creamy, slightly tangy, almost mayonnaise-like dip.

PUT all the ingredients in a food processor and blend until smooth.

If you can, leave the dip in the fridge for an hour or two to allow the flavours time to develop. Take it out of the fridge about 15 minutes before serving to return to cool room temperature.

3 adult servings

200g plain silken tofu
1 tsp cider vinegar
A scrap (about ¼ tsp) finely grated fresh ginger
A scrap (about ¼ tsp) finely grated garlic
A few drops of soy sauce
1 tbsp finely chopped mint or coriander (optional)

Red pepper & avocado dip

This is a lovely, nutritious dip with a delicately smoky flavour from the roasted pepper.

For babies: Use a good, shop-bought mayonnaise here, which will include pasteurised eggs, rather than a home-made one made with raw egg.

PREHEAT the grill to high. Grill the red pepper on a foil-lined grill pan, turning once or twice, until the skin is blackened and blistered all over. Leave to cool, then peel off the skin and remove the stalk, seeds and membranes from inside. Tear the pepper flesh roughly into pieces.

Halve, stone and peel the avocado. Put the flesh in a food processor with the red pepper and mayonnaise. Process until smooth. Season with lemon or lime juice, black pepper, and a pinch of salt if you like. Serve at cool room temperature.

3 adult servings

1 red pepper
1 ripe avocado
1 tbsp mayonnaise
A squeeze of lemon or lime juice
Freshly ground black pepper and sea salt (optional)

Courgette polpette

These vegetarian 'meatballs' are inspired by a wonderful recipe from Italian food writer Ursula Ferrigno. Her original uses aubergines, but I really like this fresh-tasting courgette version. You can easily double the quantities but you'll probably need to cook the courgette in batches.

FREEZER FRIENDLY *Freeze the uncooked polpette. Defrost before baking.*

For babies: *These make nice finger food and will introduce your baby to lots of different flavours.*

For grown-ups and older children: *Try adding a few toasted pine nuts to the mix.*

PREHEAT the oven to 200°C/gas 6. Oil a baking tray or line with a non-stick silicone liner.

Heat the oil in a large frying pan over a medium-high heat and fry the courgettes for about 10 minutes, until tender and golden. Set aside to cool a little, then combine them with all the other ingredients to make a thick, sticky mixture. Season if you like (remember that the cheeses already contain salt).

Take walnut-sized blobs of the mixture and roll into balls. Place on the baking sheet and bake for about 15 minutes, until golden.

Serve hot, warm or cold, on their own or with pitta bread (for home-made, see pages 229–31) and a tomato salad or sauce (see pages 162 and 212).

Makes about 12

2 tbsp rapeseed or olive oil
500g courgettes, finely diced
Grated zest of ½ lemon
1 egg, lightly beaten
2 generous tbsp grated Parmesan, pecorino or other well-flavoured hard cheese
½ ball of buffalo mozzarella (60–70g), diced
50g breadcrumbs
1 tbsp chopped parsley
1 garlic clove, finely chopped
Freshly ground black pepper and sea salt (optional)

Pesto

A lot of children love pesto – partly, I suspect, because bought versions are often rather salty. This recipe contains only the salt that's present in the cheese and is therefore considerably lower in salt than many commercial varieties. It's fragrant, tasty and very, very versatile.

Pine nuts are traditional, but you can use any nuts as long as you grind them finely. You can even use ground almonds, which work really well. Alternatively, you can leave out the nuts altogether and make the pesto with lightly toasted breadcrumbs instead – in which case, it might need a little more oil. You can vary the herbs as well – parsley is particularly good. Apart from being a delicious sauce for pasta, a dollop of pesto is lovely stirred into soup, in sandwiches, as an addition to salads, and alongside plain-cooked fish.

For babies: Make sure you process the nuts really finely, or try the ground almond option.

PREHEAT the oven to 180°C/gas 4. If you're using whole nuts or breadcrumbs, spread them in a small baking tray and place in the oven for 5–10 minutes, until lightly toasted – check them often as they can burn quickly. Leave to cool.

Put the toasted nuts or breadcrumbs, or ground almonds, into a food processor, along with the basil, garlic and grated cheese. Blitz to a paste, making sure all the nuts are ground finely. Then, with the motor running, slowly pour in the oil until you have a thick, sloppy purée. I normally find 100ml oil is enough but you might want a little more.

Scrape the pesto out into a bowl or jar and season with a good squeeze of lemon juice and some black pepper. This will keep, covered, in the fridge for a few days.

Makes about 200ml (enough for 3 adult portions of pasta)

50g pine nuts, almonds, walnuts or cashews, or ground almonds, or breadcrumbs

50g bunch of basil, leaves only

1 garlic clove, chopped

35g finely grated Parmesan or other mature hard cheese

About 100ml extra virgin olive oil

A good squeeze of lemon juice

Freshly ground black pepper

Corn-on-the-cob

Deliciously messy and hands-on, eating buttery corn-on-the-cob is fun – you might even find your child will eat corn this way when they won't eat the kernels on their own. Sweetcorn is a vegetable that tastes immeasurably better when it's very fresh, so try to get it soon after it's been picked.

For babies: Cut the cobs into small chunks before cooking or, if your baby has a good pincer grip, slice the kernels off after cooking. Take care as corn kernels could potentially be a choking risk for a younger baby.

FILL a saucepan large enough to accommodate the corn cobs with water (cut the cobs into pieces if you don't have a wide enough pan). Fill the pan with water and bring to the boil. Meanwhile, remove any husk and silk from the corn cobs (a great job for a young assistant).

Drop the corn cobs into the boiling water. Return to a brisk simmer and cook for 6–8 minutes, or until tender (slice a few kernels from one cob to test). Lift out the cobs with tongs or a couple of forks and drain in a colander.

While still hot, spread each corn cob with a little butter and sprinkle with some black pepper if you like. Serve as soon as the cobs are cool enough to be picked up.

Variation: **Creamed corn**
Slice the kernels from 3 corn cobs. Trim and finely slice a bunch of spring onions. Heat a knob of butter in a pan over a medium heat and gently sweat the onions for 5 minutes, then add the corn kernels and 4 tbsp water. Simmer gently, stirring once or twice, for 5–10 minutes until the corn is tender and the liquid has pretty much evaporated. Stir in 3–4 tbsp crème fraîche and simmer for another few minutes so it thickens and reduces a little. Season with pepper, and salt if you like. Serve warm, alongside simply cooked meat or fish, and some boiled or roasted new potatoes.

Per adult serving

1 corn cob
A knob of unsalted butter
Freshly ground black pepper
(optional)

Pea risotto

This is a gentle and soothing sort of dish – very easy to eat, whatever your age. It's perfect in the summer, with freshly podded peas, but you can of course make it at any time of year with frozen ones. Other veg can stand in for the peas: try broccoli, shredded lettuce or sautéed courgette cubes.

For babies: Mash or chop the finished risotto to break it down a bit if necessary – whole peas are not a good first food for young babies.

For grown-ups and older children: Add about 50ml white wine to the rice before you start adding the stock.

HEAT about half the butter in a fairly large saucepan over a medium heat. Add the onion and sweat it gently for 5–10 minutes until soft. Meanwhile, bring the stock to a low simmer in a small pan and keep it over a very low heat.

Add the rice to the onion and stir for a minute or two, so that each grain is coated in butter. Now start adding the hot stock, a ladleful at a time. Stir frequently and add a fresh ladleful of hot stock once the previous one has been absorbed by the rice.

After about 15 minutes (a bit sooner if you're using large, fresh peas), add the peas so they cook with the rice in the hot stock. After another 5 minutes, you should have added most (or all) of the stock and the rice should be cooked and tender. The consistency of the risotto should be like a very thick, ricey soup.

Turn off the heat, and dot the remaining butter over the top along with a good grating of Parmesan. Cover the pan for a minute or two so the butter melts, then stir the butter and cheese into the rice. Season if you like and serve straight away, with more Parmesan.

3 adult servings

50g unsalted butter
1 onion, finely chopped
About 1 litre chicken or
vegetable stock (see pages
236–8)
250g risotto rice
250g freshly podded peas
(about 650g unpodded
weight) or frozen peas,
defrosted
Freshly grated Parmesan,
or other mature hard cheese
Freshly ground black pepper
and sea salt (optional)

Pasta with summer tomato sauce & courgettes

Skinning and deseeding the tomatoes for this lovely fresh tomato sauce takes a little time, so it's worth making a large quantity, as suggested, and freezing the rest for other meals in smallish portions. Just add to cooked pasta, with perhaps a few peas or broccoli florets thrown in, maybe some diced cold chicken or a few tinned chickpeas, and a sprinkling of cheese.

For babies: If you use very small pasta shapes, this can be spooned. Or, to encourage your baby to feed themselves, deconstruct the dish: put pasta shapes, courgette sticks and a spoonful of sauce separately on their plate.

TO SKIN the tomatoes for the sauce, put them all in a large bowl and cover with boiling water. Leave for 1–2 minutes, or until the skins can be peeled away easily. Peel and quarter the tomatoes. Scoop out the seeds and juicy membranes into a sieve over a bowl and crush to extract the juice. Tear the tomato flesh roughly into pieces.

Heat the oil in a large, wide frying pan over a medium heat. Add the onion and garlic and cook gently for 10 minutes or until soft. Add the tomato flesh and juice. Bring to the boil, then cook at a fairly brisk simmer, stirring and crushing often, for 15 minutes or until you have a thick, mushy sauce. Transfer to a blender, add the sugar, and blitz until smooth. Season if you like. Measure 250–300ml; freeze the rest.

When ready to serve, bring a large pan of water to the boil, add the pasta and cook until done to your liking; drain.

Meanwhile, heat the oil in a small frying pan and fry the courgettes for a few minutes until turning golden brown. Add the tomato sauce and reheat. Toss into the pasta, with the basil. Stir through the mozzarella, if using. Or grate hard cheese over the pasta as you serve it.

3 adult servings, with plenty of sauce left over

For the tomato sauce
About 1.5kg large, well-flavoured tomatoes
2 tbsp rapeseed or olive oil
1 large onion, chopped
2 garlic cloves, chopped
1 tsp sugar
Freshly ground black pepper and sea salt (optional)

To serve
250g pasta shapes
1 tbsp rapeseed or olive oil
250g courgettes, diced
A few basil leaves, shredded or chopped
1 ball of buffalo mozzarella (about 125g), torn into small pieces, or grated hard cheese, to finish

Mackerel with potatoes & onions

Mackerel are a fantastic source of omega-3 fatty acids. They're in season during the summer months, and usually very cheap. Get your fishmonger to fillet them for you. Buy line-caught mackerel if you possibly can, and look out for MSC-certified fish, which comes from a completely sustainable fishery. You can also make this dish with broken-up, tinned sardines.

For babies: *Chop the finished dish or, alternatively, keep everything in fairly large chunks so they can dig in with their hands.*

PREHEAT the oven to 190°C/gas 5. If you're starting with uncooked potatoes, put them in a pan, cover with water, bring to the boil, then simmer briskly for 15 minutes or until tender. Drain well. Cut the cooked potatoes into roughly 5mm slices.

Meanwhile, heat 2 tbsp oil in a frying pan over a medium heat. Add the onion, stir to break up the rings then, once sizzling, reduce the heat to low. Cook very gently, stirring often, for about 15 minutes, till very soft, wilted and golden.

While the onion is cooking, put the mackerel fillets in a foil-lined baking dish, skin side down. Brush the flesh lightly with oil and bake for about 10 minutes or until completely opaque and flaking easily away from the skin. Use a knife and fork to flake off the flesh, checking very carefully for bones, and transfer to a dish.

Add the sliced potatoes to the soft onions, increase the heat a little and fry for another 5–10 minutes, or until both the onions and potatoes are starting to caramelise a little. Add the mackerel and use a fork to roughly crush the potatoes, onions and fish together. Season if you like, then serve hot, warm or cold, with a green salad on the side.

3 adult servings

8–10 medium new potatoes (350–400g); leftover cooked potatoes are ideal

3 tbsp rapeseed or olive oil

1 large onion, quartered and finely sliced

Fillets from 2 large or 3 small mackerel

Freshly ground black pepper and sea salt (optional)

Lamb curry

Delicately flavoured with cumin and a little fresh chilli, this is very mild, but you can always up the chilli if you want to. I usually make it with neck of lamb but you could use shoulder. The richer flavour of outdoor-reared, summer or autumn lamb is worth waiting for. If you want to make this in the spring, try it with mutton (two-year-old sheep).

FREEZER FRIENDLY

For babies: Purée or chop. If a baby's doing well with baby-led weaning, they may well be happy to pick up big chunks of meat to suck and chew.

For grown-ups: Pep up adult portions with a pinch of cayenne pepper.

HEAT 1 tbsp of the oil in a large frying pan over a fairly high heat. Add about a third of the meat (make sure you don't crowd the pan) and cook, stirring often, until browned all over. Transfer to a dish. Repeat with the rest of the lamb, adding more oil if you need it.

Meanwhile, heat 1 tbsp oil in a large casserole dish over a medium-low heat. Add the onion and sweat gently for about 5 minutes. Add the garlic and chilli and cook for a minute or two, then stir in the ginger, cumin, coriander and turmeric.

Add the lamb to the casserole, along with any juices. Add the tomatoes, stock and bay leaf. I usually add a grinding of black pepper at this stage too. Bring to the boil, then reduce the heat. Put the lid on but leave it a little askew so some steam can escape. Simmer very gently for 1½–2 hours or until the meat is really tender and the sauce reduced.

You can reduce the sauce further at the end, if you like, by removing the lid and increasing the heat for a few minutes. Add seasoning, if you like, then serve with rice.

4 adult servings

About 3 tbsp rapeseed or sunflower oil

1kg lamb neck fillet or shoulder, cut into chunks

1 large onion, finely chopped

3 garlic cloves, finely chopped

1 red chilli, deseeded and finely diced (or to taste)

1 tsp grated fresh ginger

1½ tbsp cumin seeds

1 tsp ground coriander

1 tsp ground turmeric

400g tin chopped tomatoes

500ml lamb stock (see page 218) or chicken stock (see pages 236–7)

1 bay leaf

Freshly ground black pepper and sea salt (optional)

Thyme & onion burgers

This well-flavoured meaty mixture can be formed into burgers or meatballs (large or small). Or you can fry some of it, breaking it down with a fork as you go, to make crisp meat 'crumbs' to add to pasta or scatter onto soups. The mince shouldn't be too lean – about 10 per cent fat is ideal. The burgers are lovely with a summery salad and they can be cooked outdoors on a barbecue, but of course they're good at any time of year.

FREEZER FRIENDLY *Freeze the burgers when raw. Defrost thoroughly in the fridge before cooking.*

For babies: *Burgers can be quite hard for a younger baby to chew so don't offer these until your tot has developed some chewing skills.*

HEAT 2 tbsp oil in a small frying pan over a medium heat. Add the onion and garlic and cook gently for 10–15 minutes until soft and golden. Leave to cool. Put the meat in a large bowl, add the onion, garlic and thyme, and a little seasoning if you like. Mix well with your hands. If time, leave in the fridge for an hour to develop the flavours.

With slightly wet hands, form the mixture into balls. For mini burgers, start with lumps the size of a small egg (or twice that for larger ones). Squash to form burgers no more than 2cm thick. Or, shape little walnut-sized meatballs.

To cook, heat a thin layer of oil in a large, non-stick frying pan over a medium heat. Add the burgers or meatballs and fry, turning a couple of times, for about 10 minutes until well browned on the outside and steaming hot, with no trace of pink, in the middle. Larger burgers can be barbecued.

Try the burgers in buns with ketchup and shredded lettuce or with home-made chips and pea purée (see page 106). Or combine meatballs with either of my tomato sauces (on pages 162 and 212) and serve with pasta.

Makes about 18 small burgers

Rapeseed or olive oil, for cooking

1 onion, finely chopped

1 garlic clove, finely chopped

500g minced lamb, beef, rose veal or pork

1–2 tsp chopped thyme leaves

Freshly ground black pepper and sea salt (optional)

Baked peaches

If you find yourself with a few perfectly ripe peaches or nectarines, juicy and fragrant and sweet, all you need do is slice them up, pass them round and wait for everyone to tuck in. However, if you have fruits that are a little on the firm side, this is a very nice way to soften them and intensify their flavour. Most of the peaches we eat in the UK are imported but our changing climate means some growers are beginning to produce them here. Look out for British stone fruit late in the summer.

For babies: If you're spoon-feeding, you can scoop the baked peach flesh out of the skin and crush it to a purée with a fork.

PREHEAT the oven to 180°C/gas 4. Use a little of the butter to grease a small ovenproof dish.

Place the peaches in the dish, cut sides up. Put a little nut of butter in the hollow of each. Snip the vanilla pod into little pieces and put one piece on top of each peach half. Bake, uncovered, for about 20 minutes, until the peaches are starting to caramelise on top.

Remove the pieces of vanilla pod (they should leave behind a few of their fragrant seeds). Serve the peaches warm, with any buttery juices from the dish trickled over them. A little yoghurt, cream or ice cream is very nice on the side.

2 adult servings

A knob of unsalted butter
2 peaches (or nectarines), halved, stone removed
½ vanilla pod, split open

Plum cobbler

A cobbler is a kind of fruit pudding, somewhere between a crumble and a pie, with a tender, scone-like topping. You can use other fruits here instead of plums, such as apple, berries or rhubarb.

For babies: You can mash the cobbler – perhaps loosening with a little cream – to make it easier for a younger baby to eat from a spoon. Older babies might like to use their hands.

PREHEAT the oven to 190°C/gas 5. Quarter the plums and remove their stones. Put the plums in a baking dish (I use one 20cm square). Trickle over the maple syrup, sugar or honey (not for under-ones), and scatter over the cinnamon. Toss lightly.

To make the topping, in a bowl, rub the butter into the flour with your fingertips or pulse together in a food processor, until the mixture resembles fine crumbs. Stir in the sugar. Combine the beaten egg and milk and stir lightly into the mixture to form a soft dough. Drop the dough in small dollops all over the plums (the topping won't completely cover them when raw, but will rise and spread in the oven).

Bake for about 35 minutes, or until the topping is well risen and golden brown, and a skewer pushed through it comes out clean. Serve warm, with cream or custard.

6 adult servings

1kg plums

2 tbsp maple syrup, caster sugar or honey

½ tsp ground cinnamon

For the cobbler topping

75g cold, unsalted butter, cubed

175g self-raising flour

60g caster sugar

1 egg, lightly beaten

100ml whole milk

AUTUMN
(September, October, November)

Apple muesli

This is a very simple, very scrummy breakfast – a cool alternative to a bowl of steaming porridge, but just as filling. It takes a few minutes to put together the night before, then it's all ready for you in the morning.

For babies: If you're giving this to a younger baby, you can whiz the oats in a food processor first to chop them finely. Mix the oats with apple or pear purée (see page 105) instead of grated apple.

For older children and grown-ups: Try adding seeds or nuts to the mix. I often add lightly crushed linseeds for a dose of omega-3 fatty acids.

GRATE the apple into a large cereal bowl (you don't need to peel it, but make sure there are no big bits of skin in the mix). Stir in the oats, then add enough apple juice to just cover the mixture. Give it another good stir, then cover and leave somewhere cool overnight.

If you've put the muesli in the fridge, you'll need to give it a little time to come to room temperature before serving. Uncover the bowl, stir the muesli again, then serve with a good dollop of yoghurt on top and a trickle of honey, if you like (but not for under-ones).

Per adult serving

1 medium dessert apple

About 75g porridge oats (not jumbo oats)

About 150ml apple juice

To serve
Plain, full-fat yoghurt

1 tsp honey (optional)

Cheese & apple on toast

This is quick, easy and a nice way to combine fruit with protein and carbohydrates. You can replace the apple, or combine it, with finely chopped celery or grated carrot instead.

For babies: For young babies, peel the apple before grating, or use a dollop of apple purée instead.

PREHEAT the grill to high. Toast the bread lightly and give it a thin slick of butter if you like.

Grate the apple into a bowl (you don't need to peel it, but make sure there are no big bits of skin in the mix). Add the cheese and toss to mix.

Pile the apple and cheese onto the toast. Put under the grill for a couple of minutes or until golden and bubbling. Leave to cool a little before serving.

Per adult serving

1 slice of bread

A little unsalted butter (optional)

About ½ dessert apple

About 35g Cheddar or other well-flavoured hard cheese, grated

Spaghetti squash

On the outside this simply looks like another member of the squash family, but, once cooked, the flesh breaks up rather amazingly into long strands. Eating it is a lot like eating spaghetti and you could serve it with any pasta sauce, but it's good with just a little oil or butter and a smattering of cheese and black pepper. It's one way to encourage children who like noodles or pasta to try a new vegetable. But, quite apart from that, I just love it – it's delicious. A small spaghetti squash (around 750g) will be enough for two adults, while a larger one can serve up to six, depending on what you accompany it with.

For babies: Of course you can chop this up nice and small, but even quite young babies can often figure out a way to manhandle spaghetti into their mouths (see page 53).

YOU can either boil or bake your spaghetti squash – it doesn't really matter which method you choose, the results are pretty similar. To boil, put the whole squash in a large pan, cover with boiling water from the kettle, return to the boil and cook for 30–40 minutes, until the squash feels tender all the way through when pierced with a knife or skewer. Cut it in half and scoop out the seeds, then break up the flesh into strands with a fork.

Alternatively, preheat the oven to 190°C/gas 5. Cut the squash in half and scoop out the seeds. Place, skin side down, on a greased baking sheet and bake in the oven for about 30 minutes, until the flesh can easily be separated into strands with a fork.

Either way, toss the hot strands with a little butter or oil and a sprinkling of cheese. I like some black pepper too and of course you can add a little salt if you want to. Serve as a side dish to any meat or fish. Alternatively, serve with a pasta-friendly sauce, such as pesto (see page 157), roasted veg (see page 177) or bolognese (see page 191).

2–6 adult servings, depending on size of squash

1 spaghetti squash
A little unsalted butter, or extra virgin rapeseed or olive oil
A little finely grated hard cheese
Freshly ground black pepper and sea salt (optional)

Roasted veg sauce

This pasta sauce was first cooked up with reluctant veg-eaters in mind; it's delicious – and you can use all sorts of different vegetables. Stick with the squash, making sure it's about half the volume of roasted veg, and keep in the sweet garlic, but try it with more carrots instead of the fennel, or other roots such as parsnip or beetroot, maybe a few fat, juicy tomatoes (skinned before puréeing), or even cauliflower. You could also throw in some separately roasted red pepper (skinned) at the end.

For babies: Combine the sauce with tiny pasta shapes for spoon-feeding. For baby-led weaning, cook larger pasta pieces that your baby can hold. They might prefer the sauce served separately rather than mixed in.

For grown-ups and older children: This is scrumptious with some blue cheese or diced, fried chorizo tossed in before serving.

PREHEAT the oven to 190°C/gas 5. Cut the squash half in half again and scoop out the seeds. Lay, skin-side down, at one end of a large roasting tray. Trim, core and roughly slice the fennel and add to the tray. Peel and slice the carrot and add this too, along with the unpeeled garlic cloves. Trickle a little oil over the whole lot, and give the chopped-up veg a bit of a stir. Roast for 45–55 minutes, or until everything is very tender and starting to caramelise, giving the chopped veg a stir about halfway through; cover with foil if everything seems to be browning too fast.

Scoop the flesh away from the squash skin and put into a blender with the roasted fennel and carrot. Squeeze the soft garlic cloves from their skins, and add these too. Pour in about 150ml hot stock, or milk, and blend to a thick, smooth purée. Add more stock or milk if needed and season if you like. Reheat if necessary, then serve – tossed into hot pasta, with plenty of grated cheese to sprinkle on top.

3–4 adult servings

½ butternut squash, or other squash (about 500g)

1 fennel bulb

1 large carrot

3–4 fat garlic cloves

2–3 tbsp rapeseed or olive oil

150–200ml hot chicken or vegetable stock (see pages 236–8), or hot whole milk

Freshly ground black pepper and sea salt (optional)

To serve

Freshly cooked pasta

Grated hard cheese

Carrot & lentil soup

This is a lovely, simple vegetable soup that takes advantage of the natural sweetness of carrots. A handful of red lentils thickens it and adds protein. We eat this with a variety of different toppings – garlicky croûtons, grated cheese and scraps of ham are our favourites.

FREEZER FRIENDLY

For babies: Reduce the quantity of stock or water to make a purée, rather than a soup (you can add more hot stock afterwards to thin it down for the grown-ups). You can either spoon-feed the purée, or let them dig in with their hands or some bread.

HEAT the oil in a large saucepan over a medium heat. Add the onion, garlic, celery and carrots, give it a good stir, then reduce the heat, cover the pan and leave to sweat for about 10 minutes, stirring once or twice.

When the onions are starting to soften, add the lentils and pour on the stock or water (it should just cover the veg so add a splash more if necessary). Bring to the boil, reduce the heat, cover, and simmer for 15–20 minutes until all the veg are soft.

Purée the soup in a blender, or using a hand-held stick blender. Add some seasoning if you like. Reheat if necessary. Serve scattered with some croûtons and a little grated cheese, or another topping of your choice.

3–4 adult servings

2 tbsp rapeseed or olive oil

1 onion, roughly chopped

1 garlic clove, sliced

1 celery stalk, roughly chopped

4 large carrots (about 500g), peeled and roughly sliced

About 75g red lentils

About 500ml fresh chicken or vegetable stock (see pages 236–8) or water

Freshly ground black pepper and sea salt (optional)

To serve
Croûtons
A little grated hard cheese

Helen's egg parcels

I pinched this brilliant recipe from my friend Helen, who devised it for her twin boys. Essentially little quiches without pastry, these are quick, simple and eminently adaptable. Make them once and I'm sure you'll be tweaking the recipe yourself, adding all sorts of nutritious ingredients, including leftovers. In place of the spinach mix suggested here, I often put in a few peas or some sautéed pepper or mushrooms. You can also just add a little destalked, cooked, chopped cabbage or spring greens to the onions, in place of spinach.

What you really need for these is a silicone mini-muffin mould (available from Lakeland and other cookware shops). These moulds are absolutely non-stick and make it very easy to pop out the finished parcels.

For babies: If you keep the filling ingredients chopped small, these make great finger food.

PREHEAT the oven to 200°C/gas 6.

Makes 12

Heat the oil in a small frying pan over a medium heat. Add the spring onions and cook gently for a few minutes until soft. Add the spinach and cook, stirring, until it has wilted down. Leave to cool, then chop the mixture roughly.

Lightly beat the eggs, milk or cream and melted butter in a jug or bowl to combine. Add some seasoning if you like. Pour the egg mixture into the cups of a 12-hole mini-muffin mould – each one should be about two-thirds full. Add a little of the spinach mix to each, then a little cooked fish, ham or bacon. Finish with the grated cheese. Bake for 12–15 minutes until puffed and golden.

Leave the parcels to cool a little (they will sink a bit, but don't worry), then pop out of the muffin mould. Serve warm or cold – on their own, as a snack, or with potatoes and a tomato or cucumber salad.

1 tbsp rapeseed or olive oil

A bunch of spring onions, sliced

A couple of handfuls of spinach

4 eggs, lightly beaten

A splash (1–2 tbsp) whole milk or cream

A small knob of unsalted butter, melted

A few scraps of cooked, flaked fish, or cooked, chopped ham or bacon

50g grated Cheddar or other hard cheese

Freshly ground black pepper and sea salt (optional)

Double potato pies

Sweet potato is highly nutritious, easy to cook and youngsters often love it. But, as mash, it can be quite wet, so it works best combined with standard spuds. You could also use squash or pumpkin in place of the sweet potato. These are great portable pies – perfect for picnics and packed lunches.

FREEZER FRIENDLY *Freeze the assembled but uncooked pies. Defrost completely in the fridge, then bake as below.*

For babies: *These make good finger food, but leave out the sweetcorn kernels until you're happy that your baby will be able to chew them.*

PREHEAT the oven to 190°C/gas 5. Bake both types of potatoes for about an hour, until completely tender. As soon as they are cool enough to handle, peel off the skins. Mash all the flesh together in a bowl.

Meanwhile, heat the oil in a frying pan over a medium heat. Add the onion and garlic and sauté gently for about 10 minutes, until tender. Mix this into the mashed potato, along with the cheese and sweetcorn kernels, if using.

Grease a baking sheet or line with a non-stick liner. Roll out the pastry fairly thinly on a lightly floured surface. Cut out 10 circles, 12cm in diameter, using a small plate as a guide (re-rolling and cutting from the pastry offcuts, too).

Brush the pastry rims with water. Put a heaped teaspoonful of the potato mixture on one side of each round, fold the pastry over to enclose the filling and crimp the edges firmly to seal. Brush the little pies with beaten egg to give them a glossy finish, if you like.

Put the pies on the baking sheet and bake for 20–25 minutes, until golden brown. Leave to cool on a rack, then serve warm or cold, with some green veg or salad.

Makes 10 little pies

1 medium sweet potato (about 220g)

1 medium potato (about 220g)

1 tbsp olive or rapeseed oil

½ red onion, finely chopped

1 garlic clove, finely chopped

50g Cheddar or other well-flavoured hard cheese, finely grated

About 2 tbsp fresh or frozen sweetcorn kernels (optional)

500g shortcrust or puff pastry (good-quality all-butter if using ready-made)

A little beaten egg, for glazing (optional)

Felafel

These little patties make a nutritious snack, or you can serve them for lunch with houmous, pitta bread, tomato and cucumber. You can prepare the mix and shape the felafel in advance, ready to cook later, or even the next day.

FREEZER FRIENDLY *Freeze the uncooked felafel, then defrost and cook a few at a time.*

For babies: *These are nice finger food – you can form them into little sausages, rather than patties, to make them easier to hold.*

SOAK the dried apricots in boiling water to cover for 15 minutes. Meanwhile, heat 1 tbsp oil in a small frying pan over a medium heat. Add the onion and garlic and fry gently for about 10 minutes, until soft.

Drain the apricots and put into a food processor with the onion and garlic, chickpeas, breadcrumbs, chopped herbs, orange juice and cumin. Process to a thick paste, stopping to scrape down the sides a few times. The paste should be quite smooth and well amalgamated (to ensure the felafel will hold together once cooked). Taste the paste and add some seasoning, or a touch more orange juice, if you like.

Take heaped teaspoonfuls of the mixture, roll into small balls and flatten to form little patties.

You can fry the felafel in a non-stick pan with a little oil, for a few minutes on each side, until golden brown, but I prefer to bake them in the oven, preheated to 190°C/gas 5. Brush the felafel lightly with oil and bake on a non-stick baking sheet for about 20 minutes, flipping them over halfway.

Allow to cool down before eating. Serve warm or at room temperature, with houmous, mayonnaise or another dip or sauce, as well as pitta bread and salad.

Makes about 15

5 dried apricots, roughly chopped

Rapeseed or olive oil, for cooking

1 small onion, chopped

1 garlic clove, chopped

400g tin chickpeas, drained and rinsed

50g fresh breadcrumbs

A small bunch of coriander, chopped

A small bunch of flat leaf parsley, chopped

A squeeze of orange juice

1 tsp ground cumin

Freshly ground black pepper and sea salt (optional)

Fish pâté

This simple idea is a great way to get some oily fish into the family diet. I use tinned pilchard fillets in olive oil that are sustainably caught, tasty, tender and almost without bones. The tiny bones that remain are softened by the canning process, and a whiz in the food processor renders them undetectable (they add calcium to the pâté).

You can make the pâté with tinned whole sardines or pilchards rather than fillets, but you'll need to work over them a bit more, picking out the backbones and scraping off any bits of fin and skin.

It's also very successful with fresh mackerel – just baked, flaked and processed with a dash of oil or a knob of butter.

For babies: Go for the fresh fish version, as tinned fish does contain a significant amount of salt. Serve on toast as finger food.

DRAIN off the oil from tinned fish fillets (as this takes away some of the salt too). If there's any skin on the fillets, use the tip of a small, sharp knife to scrape it off (don't worry if a few little bits remain).

If using fresh mackerel, preheat the oven to 190°C/gas 5. Put the fish fillets in a foil-lined baking dish and bake for 10–12 minutes until cooked through. Flake the flesh away from the skin, carefully removing any bones. Leave to cool.

Tip the fish fillets or flaked fresh fish into a food processor. Add the butter (or oil) and blitz to a thick paste, stopping several times to scrape down the sides of the processor. Add a squeeze of lemon or orange juice and a grinding of black pepper if you like. (If using fresh fish, you may need to add a touch more butter or oil.)

Serve the pâté on toast or oatcakes, with something fresh on the side such as cherry tomatoes, wedges of fennel or sticks of celery.

3 adult servings, as a light meal or starter

2 x 100g tins pilchard fillets in olive oil, or similar tinned oily fish fillets, or 2 large fresh mackerel fillets

25g soft unsalted butter (or 2 tbsp sunflower or rapeseed oil if you prefer)

A little lemon or orange juice
Freshly ground black pepper (optional)

Tofu salad

Tofu is an excellent vegetarian source of protein and calcium, and this delicately tangy salad is a lovely way of serving it. The recipe also works well if you replace the tofu with little cubes of paneer – Indian cheese (see page 126).

For babies: I wouldn't give this to a younger baby because the raw veg and cubes of tofu could be a choking risk. Offer it when you feel your baby is a competent chewer – try leaving the ingredients in big pieces, rather than dicing them, so they can be picked up easily.

DRAIN the tofu and pat dry with kitchen paper, then cut into dice. Combine it with the diced cucumber, red pepper and fennel.

For the dressing, whisk the ingredients together in a bowl to combine, seasoning if you like (the soy sauce will already have added some salt to the dressing).

Pour the dressing over the tofu and vegetables and toss together, then toss in the chopped coriander, if using. Serve straight away, on its own as a light meal, or with bread or a rice stir-fry.

3 adult servings, as a side dish

125g tofu

About ½ cucumber, diced

1 red pepper, diced

1 small fennel bulb, trimmed and diced

About 1 tbsp finely chopped coriander (optional)

For the dressing

½ garlic clove, crushed or finely grated

2 tsp rice vinegar

1 tsp soy sauce

2 tsp toasted sesame oil

4 tsp sunflower oil

A pinch of sugar

Freshly ground black pepper and sea salt (optional)

Fish & fennel pizza

A crisp-baked home-made pizza, topped with a few choice ingredients, is wonderful family food. In fact, you can put almost anything on a pizza and you may well find, as I do, that a small person can be tempted to try all sorts of veg presented in this way that they'd normally take issue with.

I try to keep a portion of bread dough in the freezer – once defrosted, it becomes the base for an easy pizza. We usually start with a layer of sweet, sautéed onion, but what goes on top is seldom the same twice. This combination is delicious and a good way to coax a reluctant fish-eater.

For babies: Rectangular pieces make good finger food.

3 adult servings

A portion of bread dough made with 250g flour (about ¼ of the recipe on page 230)
2 tbsp rapeseed or olive oil
1 large onion, chopped
1 fennel bulb, chopped
About 250g fish fillets, such as the fillets from 1 large mackerel, or a fat piece of white fish
A few cherry tomatoes, sliced (optional)
About 35g well-flavoured hard cheese, such as Cheddar, finely grated

HAVE the bread dough ready at room temperature. Preheat the oven to 190°C/gas 5. Meanwhile, heat the oil in a frying pan over a medium heat. Add the onion and fennel. Once sizzling, reduce the heat and cook slowly, stirring from time to time, until soft and slightly caramelised, about 15 minutes. Chop the mixture up finely, if you wish.

Put the fish fillet(s), skin side down, on a foil-lined baking tray and bake for 10–12 minutes or until cooked through. Flake the fish away from its skin, carefully removing any bones as you do so. Set the fish flesh aside.

When ready to bake the pizza, heat the oven to its highest setting. Lightly oil a baking sheet, or line with a non-stick liner. Roll out the dough on a floured surface into a round, no more than 5mm thick. Lift onto the baking sheet and roll again, stretching the dough out. Spread the onion and fennel mix evenly over the dough. Break the fish flesh into little pieces and scatter these over next. Add the sliced tomatoes, if using, then finish with the grated cheese.

Bake for about 10 minutes until the base is crisp and golden brown at the edges and the topping is golden and bubbling. Leave to cool a little, then serve in slices or fingers.

Bolognese sauce

This may not be authentic, but it is about as close as it gets to a universally liked family recipe. I always have some on hand in the freezer. It's easy to turn it into a cottage pie too: put in an ovenproof dish, top with mashed potato (see page 106), dot with a little butter, and bake at 190°C/gas 5 for about 30 minutes until golden on top and steaming hot in the middle.

FREEZER FRIENDLY

For babies: Purée or finely chop this if you're spoon-feeding a young baby.

For grown-ups and older children: Add a glass of red wine to the veg and mince and let it bubble and reduce by about half before the tomatoes go in. You can also start the dish by frying some chopped bacon or pancetta, to give an even richer result.

HEAT the oil in a large saucepan over a medium heat. Add the onion, celery, carrot and garlic. As they start sizzling, turn the heat down and cover the pan. Sweat gently for 10–15 minutes, stirring from time to time, till soft.

Add the mince to the pan, turn the heat up and stir with a fork, breaking down the chunks of mince, until all the meat is coloured and has lost its raw look. (Or you can brown the mince separately in another pan before adding it to the vegetables, if you have time.)

Add the tomatoes and bay leaf to the pan. Bring to a simmer, then half-cover the pan with the lid. Cook gently, stirring occasionally for at least 30 minutes. If you cook it for an hour, even 1½ hours, the flavour will only improve (you'll have to watch that it doesn't lose too much liquid), but it will be good after as little as 30 minutes.

Serve hot with pasta and grated cheese, or use to make cottage pie.

4–6 adult servings, with pasta or mashed potato

2 tbsp rapeseed or olive oil

1 large onion, finely chopped

1 celery stalk, finely chopped

1 large carrot, peeled and finely chopped

2 garlic cloves, finely chopped

500g beef mince (or use lamb or pork if you prefer)

2 x 400g tins chopped tomatoes

1 bay leaf

Freshly ground black pepper and sea salt (optional)

Blackberry muffins

This is a quick and easy muffin recipe and a great way to make use of even quite a small haul of blackberries. You could use other berries instead, such as blueberries, raspberries or chopped strawberries or cherries – or even dried fruit such as sultanas or chopped dried apricots. To make plum muffins, leave out the berries and scatter chopped fresh plums and a tiny sprinkling of demerara sugar over the top of each muffin before they go into the oven.

FREEZER FRIENDLY

For babies: Tear into chunks as finger food.

PREHEAT the oven to 190°C/gas 5 and put 12 large paper cases into a muffin tray.

In a large bowl, thoroughly combine the flours, baking powder, sugar and cinnamon.

In a jug, lightly beat the egg, yoghurt, milk and melted butter together to combine. Tip into the dry ingredients and mix lightly, then scatter in the blackberries and fold in until just combined.

Drop dessertspoonfuls of the mixture into the paper cases. Bake for 25–30 minutes, or until risen and golden brown.

Transfer the muffins to a wire rack. Eat on the same day you bake them – or freeze.

Makes 12

125g wholemeal or unrefined spelt flour

125g plain flour (or just use 250g plain flour if you prefer)

3 level tsp baking powder

75g caster sugar

1 tsp ground cinnamon

1 egg

125ml plain, full-fat yoghurt

125ml whole milk

75g unsalted butter, melted and slightly cooled

100–200g blackberries

Banana & sultana cake

This contains less refined sugar than standard cakes, with the banana and sultanas contributing plenty of sweetness. You can use white or wholemeal self-raising flour (though I find the wholemeal version tastes less sweet). The icing is a delicious finishing touch, but is by no means essential.

For babies: I wouldn't give this to a younger baby because of the sultanas. For older babies, leave off the icing.

GREASE and base-line a 20cm springform cake tin, or a large loaf tin (about 1 litre capacity). Preheat the oven to 180°C/gas 4.

Put the sugar, eggs and vanilla in a large bowl and whisk with an electric whisk for about 5 minutes until creamy and increased in volume. Add the oil and whisk it in, then whisk in the mashed bananas.

Combine the flour with the cinnamon, sift over the mixture (adding the bran left in the sieve, if using wholemeal) and fold in lightly. Finally, fold in the orange or lemon zest and the sultanas.

Pour the mixture into the prepared tin and bake for about 45 minutes for a round cake, or about 50 minutes for a loaf cake, until a skewer inserted into the centre comes out clean. Leave in the tin for 5–10 minutes, then transfer to a wire rack and leave to cool completely.

For the icing, if required, mix the icing sugar and orange juice together in a bowl until smooth, then trickle slowly all over the top of the cake. Stored in an airtight tin in a cool place, this cake will keep for 2–3 days.

Makes a 20cm round cake, or 1 large loaf cake

85g caster or light muscovado sugar

2 eggs

1 tsp vanilla extract

150ml sunflower oil

3 medium bananas (about 400g), the riper the better, thoroughly mashed

250g self-raising flour

1 tsp ground cinnamon

Finely grated zest of 1 orange or lemon

100g sultanas

For the icing (optional)
75g icing sugar, sifted
Juice of ½ orange

Steamed pumpkin pudding

This gently spiced pud has the tender, soft crumb that you only get with steaming. The pumpkin and apple purée lends sweetness, so less sugar is needed. You'll have more purée than you need for this recipe. Freeze the rest (for another pud), use as the base for a soup (add some stock), or offer it to your baby just as it is. It will keep in the fridge for 2 days.

For babies: Serve in chip-shaped chunks as finger food.

FOR the purée, preheat the oven to 190°C/gas 5. Cut the pumpkin or squash into wedges, scoop out the seeds and place, skin side down, in a roasting tray. Cover with foil and bake for 30 minutes. Meanwhile, peel, core and roughly slice the apples. Add to the roasting tray with the squash, re-cover and roast for a further 30 minutes, or until soft. Scoop the pumpkin flesh from the skin. Purée in a blender with the apple until smooth. Leave to cool. You should have about 500g purée; measure 200g for the pudding.

For the pudding, butter a 1 litre pudding basin. Combine the flours, cinnamon and nutmeg in a bowl. Beat the butter and sugar together in a mixing bowl until light and fluffy. Add the egg, vanilla and 1 tbsp of the flour and beat well. Gently fold in the 200g cooled pumpkin purée. Sift in the remaining flour and fold in gently, until evenly combined.

Scoop the mixture into the basin and smooth the surface. Cover the basin with a piece of pleated foil and secure with string. Stand the basin in a large saucepan, pour in boiling water to come halfway up the sides and put the lid on. Bring the water to the boil over a medium heat, then turn the heat down to a gentle simmer and steam the pudding for 1½ hours, topping up with boiling water as necessary.

Lift out the pudding basin and turn the hot pudding out onto a plate. Serve straight away, with cream or custard.

6–8 adult servings

For the pumpkin and apple purée

About 500g pumpkin or squash (a large wedge of pumpkin or ½ butternut squash)

4 dessert apples

For the pudding

100g soft unsalted butter, plus extra for greasing

100g self-raising flour

100g wholemeal self-raising flour (or just use 200g plain or wholemeal flour if you prefer)

1 tsp ground cinnamon

A good grating of fresh nutmeg

75g caster sugar

1 egg

1 tsp vanilla extract

Pear & nut smoothie

Smooth, surprisingly sweet, and full of protein, vitamins and calcium, this is lovely at any time of day. It's good for breakfast, but I also like to serve smoothies as a sort of pudding too.

Any smooth nut butter should work well but I use Equal Exchange's utterly delicious organic cashew nut butter – it's a bit of a wonder ingredient, having no sugar or salt, and tasting quite irresistible.

For babies: This could be put onto a spoon or dunked with a piece of plain toast.

PEEL, quarter and core the pear (it must be pretty ripe and tender, otherwise it won't blend). Put in a blender with the yoghurt and nut butter and blend until smooth. Serve straight away.

Per adult serving

1 ripe pear

2–3 tbsp plain, full-fat yoghurt

1 tbsp smooth, salt- and sugar-free nut butter

WINTER
(December, January, February)

Eggy bread

More elegantly known as French toast, this makes a filling breakfast. Serve it plain, or with a dusting of cinnamon, some fruit and perhaps a sprinkling of sugar.

For babies: Cut into fingers and serve without sugar.

For grown-ups and older children: Served plain, eggy bread is rather good with a crisp rasher or two of good bacon.

BEAT the egg and milk together. Lay the bread in a shallow dish (if you're making more than two slices, it's best to work in batches). Pour over the egg mixture and turn the bread, making sure it's coated all over. Leave it for a few minutes to soak up all the eggy liquid.

Meanwhile, heat the butter and oil in a non-stick frying pan over a medium heat. Transfer the soaked bread to the pan and fry for about 2 minutes, until the underside is golden brown. Flip the bread over and cook for another minute or two until the other side is golden brown. I usually cut the bread in half in the pan to check that there is no uncooked egg left in the middle.

Serve the eggy bread warm – with a little sprinkling of sugar if you like.

Per adult serving

1 egg

1 tbsp whole milk

1 thickish slice of bread

A small knob of unsalted butter

A trickle of sunflower oil

A little sugar, for sprinkling (optional)

Apple & oat muffins

Packed with good stuff, these not-too-sweet muffins are an appetising way to start the day. They're best fresh, so you might like to bake them in the evening before you go to bed. Alternatively, if you have children like mine, you can bake the muffins together ridiculously early in the morning. Often, though, I bake a batch and freeze them. A couple of muffins taken from the freezer just before I go to bed will be ready to eat by breakfast time. Sometimes I give them 5 minutes in a low oven – to make them extra nice.

I've used walnut oil here: it lends a subtle nutty taste and is a source of omega-3 fatty acids. However, if you're avoiding nuts, you can replace it with rapeseed or sunflower oil, or melted unsalted butter.

FREEZER FRIENDLY

For babies: Leave out the sultanas for very young babies (you can scoop out a couple of sultana-free portions of muffin mix, then stir in the sultanas at the last minute for everyone else's muffins).

PREHEAT the oven to 190°C/gas 5. Put 12 large muffin cases into a muffin tray.

In a large bowl, thoroughly combine both flours, the oats, baking powder, cinnamon and sugar. Add the grated apple and stir well to distribute it evenly through the mixture.

In a jug, combine the yoghurt, milk, egg and oil. Tip this into the dry ingredients and add the sultanas. Mix lightly, stopping as soon as everything is just combined.

Drop dessertspoonfuls of the mixture into the paper cases. Bake for 25–30 minutes, or until risen and golden brown.

Transfer the muffins to a wire rack. Eat within 24 hours, or freeze them.

Makes 12 muffins

100g plain flour
100g wholemeal flour, or unrefined spelt flour
50g porridge oats
3 level tsp baking powder
1 tsp ground cinnamon
50g caster sugar
2 medium dessert apples, peeled and grated
125ml plain, full-fat yoghurt
125ml whole milk
1 egg
50ml walnut oil
75g sultanas

Gill's rooty soup

This is a classic River Cottage recipe and one to which I'm very attached, because my children devour it happily. My thanks to head chef Gill Meller for letting me use it here.

FREEZER FRIENDLY

For babies: Dip toast fingers into the soup for your baby to grab.

MELT the butter in a large saucepan over a medium heat. Add the celeriac, leeks, potato, onion and garlic. Once sizzling, turn down the heat, cover and let the veg sweat gently for about 10 minutes, or until they are starting to soften.

Add the stock, bring to the boil, then lower the heat and simmer for 20–25 minutes, until the celeriac is tender.

Purée the soup in a blender, or using a hand-held stick blender. Season if you like, and reheat if necessary.

Serve the soup as it is, or topped with croûtons, grated cheese, some scraps of ham, a dollop of pesto, or whatever else takes your fancy.

6 adult servings

50g unsalted butter
1 large celeriac (about 1kg), peeled and roughly chopped
2 leeks (about 350g), trimmed and sliced
1 small potato (about 100g), peeled and diced
1 onion, chopped
2 garlic cloves, chopped
1 litre fresh vegetable or chicken stock (see pages 236–8)
Freshly ground black pepper and sea salt (optional)

Beetroot coleslaw

A coleslaw is a good way to serve up fresh fruit and veg, particularly in the winter months when root veg and cabbages are abundant and cheap. The dressing is a good opportunity to use some lovely, omega-3-rich oils such as rapeseed, and walnut too.

You can really have any combination of grated, shredded or chopped fruit and veg. Try adding some sliced red pepper, for instance, or throwing in some grated carrot instead of the apple or beetroot. Dried fruit can be included too. And you could change this yoghurt-based dressing for a dairy-free one – using olive oil and a touch of mustard and cider vinegar.

For babies: Your baby will need some chewing skills before they can tackle this dish, but you can chop the ingredients finely together to make it easier.

TO COOK the beetroot, preheat the oven to 190°C/ gas 5. Trim each beetroot and scrub well under running water. Wrap loosely in foil and bake for 1–2 hours until tender, when a knife will go through them easily. Leave to cool, then peel away the skins with your fingers or a small knife.

To make the dressing, combine the yoghurt, oil and garlic. Leave to one side while you prepare the other ingredients, so the garlic can gently infuse the yoghurt.

Grate the beetroot into a large bowl. Cut the cabbage half in half again and remove the core, then slice as thinly as you can. Now cut across the slices a few times, so you end up with quite small pieces of cabbage. Add to the beetroot. Peel and grate the apples and add to the bowl. Add the chopped parsley, if you're using it.

Toss the beetroot mixture with the dressing. Season if you like. Leave for 30 minutes or so to let the flavours mingle. Serve with cold meat, or perhaps a jacket potato and cheese. The coleslaw will keep in the fridge for 2–3 days.

3–4 adult servings, as a side dish

2 medium beetroot (about 350g)
½ small white cabbage
2 dessert apples (about 300g)
1–2 tbsp chopped parsley (optional)
Freshly ground black pepper and sea salt (optional)

For the dressing
6 tbsp plain, full-fat yoghurt
3 tbsp walnut, olive or rapeseed oil
A scrap of crushed or finely grated garlic (about ¼ clove)

Veggie bean curry

This is a great recipe to use up odds and ends of veg – root veg, peppers, frozen peas or beans, broccoli. squash or pumpkin, mushrooms etc, can all play a part. And it's fine to use a ready-made, low-salt stock.

For babies: Go easy on the chilli or leave it out. Chop or purée the dish before serving. Alternatively, select some nice big chunks of veg that your baby can pick up. Take care with the whole beans or chickpeas as these could potentially be a choking hazard.

HEAT the oil in a large saucepan over a medium heat. Add the cumin seeds and fry gently for a minute or two, then add the onion. Let it sweat for about 10 minutes, until soft, then add the garlic, ginger, chilli and turmeric. Cook, stirring well, for a minute or so.

Tip the tomatoes into the pan, stir and bring to the boil, then reduce to a simmer. Cook, uncovered, stirring often and crushing the bits of tomato with a fork, for 15–20 minutes, until the mixture reduces and thickens. (I normally use this time to prepare the veg that's about to go in.)

Add the mixed veg, beans or chickpeas and stock to the saucepan. Return to a gentle simmer and cook for around 45 minutes, stirring often, until the veg are tender and the sauce is thick and rich. If you're using any tender veg, such as broccoli or peas, add them towards the end of the cooking time.

Stir in the garam masala, the yoghurt or cream if using, and add a pinch of sugar, some pepper and some salt too, if you like. Serve with rice.

3 adult servings

2 tbsp rapeseed or sunflower oil

1 heaped tsp cumin seeds

1 onion, chopped

1 garlic clove, grated

A small knob of fresh ginger, grated

½ red chilli, deseeded and finely chopped (optional, or more if you like)

1 heaped tsp turmeric

400g tin chopped tomatoes

A couple of handfuls (about 250g) of mixed chopped veg (see above)

400g tin white beans or chickpeas, drained and rinsed

400ml vegetable stock (see page 238)

1 tsp garam masala

2–3 tbsp plain, full-fat yoghurt, or cream (optional)

Freshly ground black pepper, sugar and sea salt (optional)

Brussels sprouts gratin

This is simply the cauliflower cheese treatment, applied to Brussels sprouts. Of course you can replace the sprouts with a medium-large cauliflower, cut into florets: cook in boiling water for about 5 minutes, or until just tender.

For babies: Chop up unless your baby is happy to dig in with their hands.

FOR the sauce, put the milk in a saucepan with the onion, bay leaf and peppercorns. Bring to just below the boil, take off the heat and set aside to infuse for half an hour or so. Preheat the oven to 190°C/gas 5.

Strain the milk and discard the flavourings. Melt the butter in a small saucepan until foaming. Stir in the flour and cook, stirring, over a low heat for a couple of minutes. Take off the heat. Add a splash of the warm milk and stir vigorously with a spatula or small whisk, keeping the mixture smooth. Keep adding the milk in this way and you should achieve a smooth sauce. Return to the heat and bring to a gentle simmer, stirring. Cook for a couple of minutes, stirring often, so the sauce thickens. Remove from the heat and stir in the cheese and mustard. Season with pepper. Cover the surface closely with clingfilm to stop a skin forming, and set aside while you prepare the sprouts.

Trim the sprouts, then cut across into roughly 5mm slices (or quarter them vertically if you prefer). Bring a large pan of water to the boil. Drop in the sprouts and, once the water returns to a simmer, cook for 2 minutes. Drain well.

Combine the sprouts with the sauce and spread in a gratin dish (about 25 x 15cm, or 20cm square). Mix the cheese with the breadcrumbs and sprinkle over the top. Bake for about 25 minutes until bubbling and golden. I like to eat this with a baked potato, sometimes some poached chicken too.

4 adult servings

500g Brussels sprouts

For the cheese sauce
300ml whole milk
1 small onion, roughly chopped
1 bay leaf
A few black peppercorns
25g unsalted butter
25g plain flour
100g well-flavoured hard cheese, such as Cheddar, grated
1 tsp Dijon mustard
Freshly ground black pepper

For the topping
30g well-flavoured hard cheese, such as Cheddar, grated
30g fairly coarse breadcrumbs

Spelt with leeks & squash

This is a comforting dish, rather similar to a risotto, but using wonderful, nutty grains of spelt instead of rice.

For babies: *Chop or mash to make this spoonable.*

For grown-ups and older children: *Try adding blue cheese at the end.*

PREHEAT the oven to 190°C/gas 5. Peel and deseed the squash, and cut the flesh into bite-sized chunks. Put in a roasting dish and toss with 2–3 tbsp oil. Loosely wrap the whole garlic cloves in a scrap of foil, and place on top of the squash (the foil stops the garlic burning). Roast for about an hour, until the squash is tender and starting to caramelise, giving it a stir halfway through.

When the squash is about halfway through its cooking time, heat the butter and another 1 tbsp oil in a large saucepan over a medium heat and add the sliced leeks. As soon as they start to sizzle, turn the heat down low, cover the pan and let them sweat gently for around 10 minutes, stirring once or twice, until soft.

Add the spelt, thyme or sage, and all but a ladleful of the stock to the leeks. Bring to a simmer, cover and cook gently for 25 minutes, stirring every now and again, until tender.

When the squash is cooked, remove the little parcel of garlic from the tin. Unwrap it and squeeze the soft garlic cloves out of their skins. Mash them, or blitz in a blender, with the reserved stock, then add to the simmering spelt.

When the spelt is cooked, turn off the heat and stir in the grated cheese. Finally, stir in the roasted squash. Season if you like (remember that the cheese will contribute some salt). Serve straight away.

3 adult servings

1kg squash, such as butternut or crown prince

3–4 tbsp rapeseed or olive oil

4 garlic cloves (unpeeled)

A knob of unsalted butter

2 leeks, trimmed and thinly sliced

150g pearled spelt

1 tsp chopped thyme or sage

500ml chicken or vegetable stock (see pages 236–8)

25g well-flavoured hard cheese, such as Cheddar, grated

Freshly ground black pepper and sea salt (optional)

Roasted roots

Fat fingers of sweet, roasted root veg are ideal food for baby-led weaners – and delicious for everyone else too. I've suggested making a roasted garlic relish for older family members, but you could just as easily use pesto, some crumbled blue cheese or a tomatoey chutney to give that zing.

For babies: Serve the veg as it is (without the relish). Perhaps put some plain pasta pieces and grated cheese alongside – great for self-feeding.

For grown-ups and older children: Serve the garlic relish (or alternative).

PREHEAT the oven to 190°C/gas 5. Peel the root veg (if using parsnips, remove any core) and cut them all into fat fingers – at least 8–9cm long and 2–3cm in width if you're planning to offer these as finger food. Put the veg in a large roasting dish and toss with the oil. If using garlic, slice the top off it so the flesh is just revealed. Wrap the head loosely in foil and add to the dish with the prepared veg. Roast for about 1 hour, giving the veg a stir halfway through. You want everything to be tender and slightly caramelised, but not so soft that it's all falling apart.

If you've roasted garlic, keep the veg warm while you prepare the relish. Squeeze the soft garlic out of the papery skins and drop it into a mortar. Crush to a smooth purée with the pestle. Add the lemon zest, mustard and honey, and some seasoning if you like, and beat to a smooth consistency. Taste and add more mustard or honey if you think it is needed. Serve the relish alongside the veg (but not for under-ones as it contains honey).

Roasted veg is a great accompaniment to simple meat and fish such as lamb shanks (see page 218), roast chicken (see page 139) or baked and flaked fish (see page 239), or you can toss it into freshly cooked pasta, adding the relish for older family members and sprinkling with grated cheese.

3 adult servings, as a side dish

About 1kg mixed root vegetables, such as carrots, parsnips, potatoes and sweet potatoes

2 tbsp rapeseed or olive oil

1 whole head of garlic (optional)

To complete the relish

Grated zest of 1 small lemon

1 tsp Dijon mustard

1 tbsp clear honey

Freshly ground black pepper and sea salt (optional)

Fish pasta al forno

A lovely alternative to fish pie, this pasta bake is a great way to introduce your child to all sorts of fish – almost any, except oily fish like mackerel, which doesn't quite work with a white sauce. I like a mixture of white fish, salmon (organic) and a smattering of cold-water prawns. The dish includes vegetables too: I've used carrot and leek but you could add anything you like, such as chopped spinach or kale, or chopped green beans or broccoli if you're making this in the summer.

There are several different components to the dish, but you don't have to make it all in one go. The leeks can be cooked, the fish chopped then refrigerated, and the white sauce made well ahead of time.

For babies: Chop the finished dish if you need to. If your baby has never eaten shellfish or fish before, you should introduce them one at a time, not together, just in case there's any kind of reaction.

For grown-ups and older children: Once your children are a little older, try including some smoked fish in the mix.

FOR the sauce, put the milk, onion, bay leaf and peppercorns in a saucepan and bring to just below boiling point. Set aside to infuse while you prepare the fish and vegetables.

Lightly butter an ovenproof dish (I use one 20cm square). Preheat the oven to 190°C/gas 5.

Heat the oil in a frying pan over a medium-low heat. Add the leek and garlic and cook gently for 10 minutes or so, stirring from time to time, until soft. Remove from the heat and set aside.

Cut the fish fillets off the skin. Check the fillets carefully for small bones and remove any you come across with kitchen tweezers. Cut the flesh into small chunks. Combine with any cooked shellfish you are using.

3 adult servings

A little butter, for greasing
1 tbsp olive or rapeseed oil
1 leek, trimmed and finely sliced
1 garlic clove, chopped
About 400g mixed raw fish and cooked shellfish, such as fillets of pollack, haddock and salmon, and some cooked prawns or mussels (see page 133)
175g pasta shapes, such as macaroni, fusilli or conchiglie
1 medium carrot, peeled and finely chopped

To make the sauce, strain the warm milk and discard the flavourings. Melt the butter in a small saucepan until foaming. Stir in the flour to make a smooth paste (a roux). Cook, stirring, over a low heat for a couple of minutes. Remove from the heat. Add a splash of the warm milk and stir vigorously with a spatula or small whisk, keeping the mixture smooth. Add a dash more and stir again. Keep adding the milk in this way and you should achieve a smooth sauce, the consistency of single cream.

Return to the heat and bring to a gentle simmer, stirring often. Cook for a couple of minutes, stirring often, so the sauce thickens. Remove from the heat and stir in the parsley and mustard. Season if you like. If you're making this a few hours ahead, cover the surface closely with clingfilm to stop a skin forming, and set aside.

Bring a pan of water to the boil. Add the pasta and chopped carrot and cook for a minute or two less than recommended on the pasta packet, so it is marginally underdone. Drain well.

Combine the pasta, white sauce and leek mixture. Fold in the fish and transfer to the baking dish. Combine the breadcrumbs and cheese and sprinkle over the top. Bake for about 25 minutes, until the top is golden, the sauce bubbling and the bake is steaming hot right through to the centre. Serve with lightly buttered peas or spinach.

For the sauce
350ml whole milk
1 small onion, roughly chopped
1 bay leaf
A few black peppercorns
20g unsalted butter
20g plain flour
1 tbsp finely chopped parsley
1 tsp Dijon mustard
Freshly ground black pepper and sea salt (optional)

For the topping
40g fresh breadcrumbs
50g Cheddar or other well-flavoured hard cheese, grated

Baked fish with winter tomato sauce

This sauce – rich and tomatoey with a hint of sweet-and-sourness – is a winner, and very nice with fish. I call it winter tomato sauce as it's made with tinned tomatoes, but of course you can make it at any time of the year and use it as you wish. It can be served with chicken, roasted vegetables or pulses; it's excellent on pasta with a little broccoli, shredded kale or mushrooms; it's nice cold, too, as a kind of relish or dip. It's also one of those recipes that tastes even better the day after you make it.

FREEZER FRIENDLY

For babies: Chop or mash the fish and sauce together.

TO MAKE the tomato sauce, heat the oil in a large saucepan over a medium-low heat. Add the onion and garlic and sweat gently for about 10 minutes until soft. Transfer to a blender and add the tomatoes, apple juice, cider vinegar and mixed spice. Blitz until smooth.

Return the sauce to the pan, add the bay leaf and bring to the boil, then turn the heat down. Simmer fairly briskly, uncovered, for about 30 minutes, stirring from time to time, until the sauce is reduced by at least half and tastes tangy, sweet and rich. Season if you like.

Meanwhile, cook the fish. Preheat the oven to 190°C/gas 5. Put the fish fillets on a foil-lined baking tray and brush with a little oil. Bake for 12–15 minutes, or until cooked through and flaking easily from the skin (really thick hunks of fish might take a little longer).

Serve at once, with a few good spoonfuls of the hot sauce. Accompany with home-made chips, jacket potato or polenta 'chips' (see page 240) and a green vegetable, if you like.

3 adult servings

3 fillets of white fish, such as pollack, whiting or sustainably caught haddock or cod (see page 23)

For the tomato sauce
2 tbsp rapeseed or olive oil
1 onion, roughly chopped
1 garlic clove, roughly chopped
400g tin chopped tomatoes
75ml apple juice
½ tsp cider vinegar
A pinch of ground mixed spice
1 bay leaf
Freshly ground black pepper and sea salt (optional)

Venison stew with herb dumplings

Venison is a wonderful rich-but-lean meat, in season during the autumn and winter. You should be able to get it from any good butcher. Go for chunks of venison neck and/or shoulder, or 'stewing venison'. The dish is equally good made with an economical beef cut, such as stewing steak or shin of beef. If using shin, cook the stew for longer, up to 3 hours. If you happen to have some good beef or chicken stock to hand, use it, but water alone is fine.

FREEZER FRIENDLY *Any leftover stew (minus the dumplings) can be frozen in small portions, then defrosted and reheated for a quick supper.*

For babies: *You can purée or chop up the stew to make it spoonable. Alternatively, if your baby's doing well with baby-led weaning, they may be happy to pick up big chunks of meat and veg for themselves.*

For grown-ups and older children: *Deglaze the meat-browning pan with a glass of red or white wine, for a slightly richer stew.*

PREHEAT the oven to 140°C/gas 1.

Heat 1 tbsp of the oil in a large ovenproof casserole over a medium heat. Add the bacon and, once the fat starts to run, add the onions and garlic. Lower the heat and cook gently, stirring occasionally, until the onions are soft and golden.

Put the flour on a plate, add the meat and toss in the flour. In a large frying pan, heat 1 tbsp oil over a fairly high heat. Take a third or half of the meat, shake off any excess flour, then brown the meat in the frying pan, getting it good and crusty all over. Transfer it to the casserole with the onions. Repeat with the remaining meat, adding more oil as needed. It's important to do this in 2 or 3 batches so as not to crowd the pan, which makes it hard to brown the meat properly.

5–6 adult servings

About 3 tbsp olive or rapeseed oil

100g unsmoked streaky bacon or pancetta, in small cubes or ribbons

2 onions, finely sliced

2 garlic cloves, sliced

2 tbsp plain flour

1kg venison neck and/or shoulder or stewing steak, cut into chunks

2 carrots, sliced

2 celery stalks, sliced

When all the meat is browned and added to the casserole dish, deglaze the frying pan by tipping in half a glass of water. Let it bubble and fizz for a minute or two, scraping up any caramelised bits of meat stuck to the pan, then tip the whole lot into the casserole. Add the carrots and celery to the casserole and stir well.

Stir the Worcestershire sauce and tomato purée into 500ml just-boiled water. Pour this over the meat and veg – it should just cover everything. If not, add a little more water. Add the herbs. Bring the liquid to the boil, cover the pan and transfer to the oven. Cook for about 1½ hours.

When the meat's been in the oven for nearly 1½ hours, make the dumplings. Mix the flour, suet and herbs thoroughly in a bowl. Season with pepper, and salt if you like (they really benefit from a pinch). Add enough cold water to make a soft, slightly sticky dough – about 100ml. With well-floured hands, break the dough into walnut-sized chunks, and roll each into a round dumpling.

Take the stew from the oven, give it a stir and add some seasoning if you like. Arrange the dumplings on top, then return to the oven, uncovered. Increase the heat to 180°C/ gas 4 and cook for 30 minutes, or until the dumplings are risen, golden and cooked through. Serve piping hot with shredded greens, and mashed potato if you like.

Alcohol in cooking

There's a common misunderstanding that when wine, beer or spirits are cooked, all their alcohol is 'burned off'. Certainly some of the alcohol evaporates, but not all. Even a slow-cooked stew, simmered for several hours, can still retain very small amounts of alcohol. I do not believe that a splash of wine used to deglaze a pan or added in the early stages of a risotto would do a child any harm – but you might want to avoid adding wine to a dish for a baby of 12 months or younger.

1 tsp Worcestershire sauce

1 tbsp concentrated tomato purée

1 bay leaf

1 thyme sprig

Freshly ground pepper and sea salt (optional)

For the herb dumplings

175g self-raising flour

75g shredded suet

1 tbsp finely chopped herbs of your choice (rosemary is my favourite here)

Little toads in-the-hole

I've tried making this as individual toady puddings in muffin tins – but you don't get the right ratio of crisp-outside to tender-inside with the batter. This is much better, I think: small chunks of sausage in a generous Yorkshire pudding blanket that you can cut or tear and share around.

If you want something unprocessed and salt-free, use little home-made meatballs (see burger recipe on page 167) instead of sausages.

For babies: Sausages can be quite hard for a younger baby to chew, so chop them finely. A chunk of Yorkshire pud, on the other hand, is great finger food.

TO MAKE the batter, whiz all the ingredients together in a food processor. Alternatively, put the flour into a bowl, whisk the eggs, egg whites and milk together, then pour them into the flour and gradually whisk in the dry flour until you have a smooth batter. Leave the batter to rest for at least half an hour, up to 2 hours, before using.

Preheat the oven to 220°C/gas 7. Pour the oil, or a little goose fat, into a baking tin, about 20 x 25cm. Snip each sausage into 3 or 4 pieces and put in the tin. Bake in the oven for 10 minutes.

Meanwhile, give the batter another quick whisk. Remove the sausages from the oven then, quickly, while the fat is still spitting hot, pour the batter into the tin. Quickly return to the oven. Bake for a further 20 minutes, or until the Yorkshire pudding is puffed up and golden brown.

Serve with mashed potato and a green vegetable, such as chopped cabbage.

4 adult servings

2 tbsp rapeseed or olive oil, or goose fat

6 sausages

For the batter
150g plain flour
2 eggs, plus 2 egg whites
200ml whole milk

Very simple lamb shanks

This is an easy way to cook lamb shanks, which are inexpensive, meaty little joints from the rear leg of the animal. You end up with tender chunks of moist meat – great for babies doing baby-led weaning – and a tasty pool of lamb stock that you can use in another recipe.

For babies: Offer long pieces of the tender meat for hand-grabbing, or chop it up and mix with some of the sauce, for spooning.

PREHEAT the oven to 140°C/gas 1.

2 generous adult servings

Choose a casserole dish or lidded ovenproof pan, small enough to hold the lamb shanks fairly snugly. Heat the oil in the dish over a fairly high heat. Add the shanks and brown well all over, giving them a few minutes on each surface so they start to form a good, golden brown crust.

Add the onion, carrot, celery, bay leaf and garlic to the pan and immediately pour on enough water to come about halfway up the lamb shanks – probably about 500ml. Make sure all the veg is immersed in the liquid. Let the liquid come up to the boil, then put the lid on the pan and transfer to the oven. Cook for 2 hours, taking the pan out halfway through and turning the shanks over in the liquid.

To serve, give a shank to each adult, or pull the tender chunks of meat off the bone for smaller diners. You can eat the butter-soft vegetables too, along with a spoonful or two of the stock (use the rest of the stock for another dish, such as lamb curry (see page 165). Serve some freshly cooked veg too – try champ-cannon (see page 120) or some roasted carrots and parsnips.

2 tbsp olive or rapeseed oil

2 lamb shanks

1 large onion, roughly chopped

1 carrot, roughly chopped

1 celery stalk, roughly chopped

1 bay leaf

2 garlic cloves, peeled and lightly squashed

Pork & apple hash

This is a good way to use up leftovers after a roast pork dinner, but it's so delicious I would cook the ingredients from scratch – maybe baking a potato and roasting a couple of pork belly strips at the same time.

For babies: Your baby will need some chewing skills before tackling pork, but you can chop it up very finely to make it easier. Stir a little stock or apple juice in at the end of cooking to make a softer mix if you like.

HEAT the oil in a large frying pan over a medium heat. Add the apple and sage and fry for 5–10 minutes or until the apple has started to soften and caramelise a little. Add the potato and fry for another 5–10 minutes, tossing it with the apple and crushing them together a bit.

Meanwhile, chop the pork. If you are serving the dish to a younger baby, chop it finely. Older diners can, of course, have bigger chunks.

When the potato has started to take on some colour, add the pork to the pan. Cook for another few minutes, until the pork is hot and everything has come together into a lovely golden hash. Serve hot, perhaps with some green salad on the side.

3 adult servings

2 tbsp rapeseed or olive oil (or fat from roasting pork)

1 dessert apple, peeled, cored and sliced

About 1 tsp chopped sage (optional)

About 200g cooked potato (baked, boiled or roasted)

About 150g cooked pork

Baby baked apples

This is such a simple little pudding, and quite delicious. It takes a while to cook, but the preparation time is minimal.

For babies: You can leave out the syrup (don't give a baby honey). Mash or roughly chop the soft apple and sultanas for spooning, or just break the apple into pieces, let it cool and encourage your baby to dig in. Avoid giving sultanas or pieces of apple skin to a young baby.

PREHEAT the oven to 180°C/gas 4.

Cut a thin slice off the base of each apple so they will stand up easily. Score a line through the skin around the equator of the apples to stop the skin bursting. Use an apple corer to remove the cores, making sure you take out every bit of the fibrous centre – you might have to push the corer through 2 or 3 times to do this.

Stand each apple on a piece of foil in a baking dish. Pack a good pinch of sultanas or raisins into the cavity of each. Press the knob of butter on top, pushing it down with your finger, then carefully pour in the honey (not for under-ones) or syrup. Bring the foil loosely up around each apple to enclose it.

Bake for 35–45 minutes, or until the apple flesh feels soft when pierced with a knife; the time will vary depending on the size and variety of apple. Transfer to serving dishes, making sure you add the caramelised juices too.

To eat, use a spoon and fork to break open the apple and mash the flesh together with the sultanas and sweet juices. A little cold cream is a wonderful accompaniment.

Per adult serving

1 dessert apple

A pinch of sultanas or raisins

A small knob of unsalted butter

1 tsp honey or maple syrup

Apricot & orange loaf

Many moons ago, I came across a fantastic recipe for 'Molly Cake', from the tearooms at Cliveden. This fruit-packed loaf is based on that recipe. Dairy- and egg-free, it has no refined sugar, just dried fruit. A small slice will keep anyone going for hours.

For babies: This is very sweet with lots of chunky bits of fruit so I'd avoid giving it to a young baby.

PREHEAT the oven to 170°C/gas 3. Line a large loaf tin (about 1 litre capacity) with baking parchment.

Use kitchen scissors to roughly chop the apricots and dates and put them in a small pan. Finely grate the zest of one of the oranges and add to the pan.

Squeeze the juice from both oranges into a measuring jug, then top up with water to come to 350ml. Add this liquid to the dried fruit in the pan. Bring to the boil, then remove from the heat and set aside.

Combine the flours, baking powder, spice, ground almonds and sultanas or raisins in a large bowl. Add the soaked apricots and dates, with their liquid, and mix thoroughly.

Scoop the mixture into the prepared tin and gently smooth out. Bake for about 45 minutes, or until a skewer inserted into the middle comes out clean.

Leave in the tin for 5–10 minutes, then transfer to a wire rack to cool. Store the cake in an airtight tin, where it will keep for several days.

Makes at least 10 slices

100g dried apricots
100g stoned dates
2 oranges
125g plain flour
100g unrefined spelt flour or wholemeal flour
2 tsp baking powder
1 tsp ground mixed spice, or just ground cinnamon
50g ground almonds
375g sultanas or raisins

Sultana buns

These little buns are gently sweetened with apple juice and sultanas, rather than refined sugar. You can make them all white, or with some wholemeal flour. Either way, they're lovely fresh from the oven, torn into pieces for nibbling. Alternatively, if they're more than a day old, split them, then toast and spread with a little butter. They also freeze well.

FREEZER FRIENDLY

For babies: Thick slices of these make good finger food but, because of the sultanas, don't give them to a young baby.

HEAT the milk until steaming in a small pan, then take off the heat. Add the butter and leave until it has melted and the milk is warm rather than hot.

In a large bowl, thoroughly combine the flours, yeast, spice, sultanas and orange zest. Make a well in the centre, pour in the warm milk and butter, apple juice and beaten egg and quickly mix together to form a rough, sticky dough.

Turn out onto a lightly floured surface and knead for 5–10 minutes, until smooth. If sultanas pop out, just knead them back in. Put the dough in a clean bowl and cover with a tea towel. Leave in a fairly warm, draught-free place until doubled in size – at least an hour. Meanwhile, grease and lightly flour a baking tray, or line with a non-stick liner.

Turn the dough out onto a lightly floured surface and deflate with your fingers. Cut into 12–16 pieces, gently shape into buns and place on the baking tray. Leave for 30–60 minutes until doubled in size. Preheat the oven to 200°C/gas 6.

Brush the buns with beaten egg or milk and bake for 15–20 minutes until puffed and golden brown. Transfer to a wire rack to cool. Eat while still warm, or let cool completely.

Makes 12–16

125ml whole milk
50g unsalted butter
250g plain white flour
250g strong white bread flour, or wholemeal bread flour, or unrefined spelt flour
2 level tsp easy-blend yeast
1 heaped tsp ground mixed spice
200g sultanas
Finely grated zest of 1 orange
125ml apple juice
1 egg, beaten
A little beaten egg or milk, for glazing

Chocolate & almond cookies

These indulgent choccy biccies are testament to my fervent belief that no food is 'bad' and nothing should be forbidden. They use rich dark chocolate (buy the best you can afford) and include ground almonds, which increase their nutrient value and make them temptingly chewy. If you're avoiding nuts, however, you can simply replace the ground almonds with more plain flour. Quite delicious on their own, these are also good with something creamy such as frozen yoghurt, ice cream or a fruit fool.

For babies: With their crumbly texture and sugary taste, I wouldn't give these cookies to a young baby.

LINE two baking sheets with baking parchment or non-stick liners (or use one baking sheet and bake in two batches). Preheat the oven to 170°C/gas 3.

Put the chocolate in a bowl and place it inside another, larger, bowl half-filled with just-boiled water. Leave the chocolate to melt, stirring from time to time. Allow to cool a little, so it's no more than blood temperature.

Meanwhile, beat the butter and sugar together for a few minutes until light and fluffy. Add the melted chocolate and vanilla and beat in briefly. Combine the flour and ground almonds and add to the mixture. Work together with a fork to form a soft dough.

Put heaped teaspoonfuls of the dough onto the baking sheet, spacing them well apart as they'll spread in the oven. Bake for 15 minutes. At this point they'll still be very soft, so let them cool a little on the tray.

When ready, carefully transfer the cookies to a wire rack to cool and firm up. Store in an airtight tin for up to 4 days.

Makes 20–25

100g dark chocolate (at least 70 per cent cocoa solids), broken into chunks

125g unsalted butter, softened

125g caster sugar

½ tsp vanilla extract

100g plain flour

100g ground almonds

ALL YEAR ROUND

Basic bread

This recipe contains a proportion of wholegrain flour, but not too much (see page 59); you can increase the percentage as your children get older. It also has a little plain flour, for softness. The result is a really versatile dough that you can use to make a large loaf for slicing, but also pitta breads, bread sticks or pizza bases. Both the raw dough and the finished bread freeze well.

This is not a low-salt bread recipe, because I don't think low-salt bread tastes very nice. It contains somewhere in the region of 0.7g salt per 100g (roughly two slices), which is still a lot lower than many commercial breads.

Personally, I would rather bake this and make sure my children don't eat it at every meal, than have us all chow down breakfast, lunch and tea on something bland. Having said that, I used to make my daughters salt-free breadsticks when they were babies, which were excellent for chewing practice and dipping into things.

You can, of course, reduce the salt in this yourself if you'd prefer, or leave it out altogether – it's entirely up to you.

FREEZER FRIENDLY *To freeze the uncooked dough, allow it to rise, then knock it back. Cut it into appropriate sized pieces, for a loaf, pitta breads, breadsticks etc, then immediately dust with flour, wrap in clingfilm and freeze. Allow the dough to defrost, give it a little knead, then let it rise again before baking.*

For grown-ups and older children: *Add a handful of seeds to the dough for a particularly nutritious loaf.*

(recipe overleaf)

PUT the flours, yeast, sugar and salt in a large bowl and combine thoroughly. Make a well in the centre and add the oil, then pour in 625ml warm water. Mix to a rough dough in the bowl. You may feel you need more water – different flours vary a lot in absorbency – you are aiming for a dough that feels quite sticky and squidgy when you squash it between your fingers.

Turn out the dough onto a lightly floured surface and knead it for 5–10 minutes. Hold one end of the dough down with one hand, then stretch the rest away from you along the worktop with the other. Fold the dough back on itself, and repeat, turning the dough 90° every few stretches. Kneading should be a fairly gentle, rhythmic process that folds air into the dough and stretches the gluten within it, rather than a vigorous pummelling!

When the dough feels smooth, form it into a ball. Put a little oil into a large, clean bowl, add the dough and turn it so it's covered in a light film of oil. Cover with clingfilm and leave in a fairly warm, draught-free place until doubled in size – probably about an hour, but possibly longer.

Scoop the dough out of the bowl onto a lightly floured surface. Use your fingers to 'knock it back', or deflate it. Cut into two equal pieces. Shape the first piece into a loaf – I favour a simple round loaf that I put straight onto a lightly floured baking tray or into a well-floured proving basket, but you can use a loaf tin if you prefer. Dust the dough with flour, cover lightly with a cloth or clingfilm and leave in a fairly warm, draught-free place until doubled in size again.

Shape the second piece into another loaf, if you like, or use it to make other bready goodies (see right).

While the dough is proving, preheat your oven to its highest temperature – this is 250°C/gas 10 for me.

Makes 2 loaves, or 1 loaf, plus breadsticks, pittas or 2 pizza bases

500g strong white bread flour

250g strong wholemeal bread flour, or unrefined spelt flour

250g plain white flour

2 tsp easy-blend yeast

2 tsp sugar

10g (1½ level tsp) fine sea salt

2 tbsp olive or rapeseed oil, plus a little for oiling

When the dough has risen, use a very sharp knife to slash the top a few times. Transfer it quickly to the oven and bake for 10 minutes. Then reduce the heat to 200°C/gas 6 and bake for a further 20 minutes, or until golden brown on top.

To test, hold the loaf upside down in a cloth in your hand and knock on the base. You should feel the loaf vibrating in your hand, and it should sound hollow; if not, return it to the oven for a little longer. Once cooked, leave the bread to cool completely on a wire rack before slicing.

Variations

For each of the following, prepare the bread dough, leave to rise and then knock back, following the method on the opposite page.

Breadsticks After knocking back, take walnut-sized pieces of dough and roll them out into long, thin rods. Place on a lightly greased baking tray. Leave to rise for 10–15 minutes, then bake at 200°C/gas 6 for about 10 minutes. Leave to cool on a wire rack. These are great to keep in the freezer as they defrost within minutes.

Pitta breads Take egg-sized balls of knocked-back dough. Roll them out on a floured surface into oval shapes, no more than 5mm thick. Transfer to a greased tray and leave for 10–15 minutes, then bake at 220°C/gas 7 for about 8 minutes, until puffed up and just starting to brown. Take them from the oven and immediately wrap in a clean tea towel. Leave to cool completely before unwrapping (the trapped steam keeps the pittas soft).

Pizza bases For a large pizza that will provide 3 adult servings, use a quarter of the knocked-back dough. Leave it to rest for 10 minutes, then roll it out on a floured surface until no more than 5mm thick. Transfer to a greased baking sheet (it will shrink back a bit when you transfer it, so give it a bit more rolling, pushing and stretching when on the baking sheet). Add your chosen toppings and bake at your oven's maximum temperature for 10–12 minutes.

Soda bread

This is the quickest, easiest way to produce yummy bread for your family, and the recipe is endlessly adaptable. Increase the amount of wholegrain flour as your child matures (see page 59), or try adding some herbs, grated cheese or seeds (not large seeds for babies). Or leave out the salt and add chopped dried fruit, a pinch of spice and a little sugar to make a lovely tea bread.

FREEZER FRIENDLY

For babies: Chunky slices are good as finger food.

PREHEAT the oven to 200°C/gas 6. Lightly grease a baking tray, or line with a non-stick liner.

Put the flour, bicarbonate of soda and salt in a large bowl and use a whisk to thoroughly combine. Stir the yoghurt and milk together, then add to the dry ingredients and mix well. This will produce a sticky dough (much stickier than other soda bread doughs you might have made), which I find produces a lovely, moist loaf that keeps well.

You can shape the dough with well-floured hands if you like, but I prefer to simply scrape it onto the baking tray in a big mound, then shape it roughly with a spatula, leaving the surface nice and textured. If you want to make rolls, scoop small portions of the dough onto a well-floured work top. Roll them in flour and form into rough bap shapes before transferring to the baking sheet.

Bake for about 45 minutes (20 minutes for small rolls), until well risen and golden brown. Leave on a rack to cool.

You can slice the bread while still warm, or leave it to cool completely. Keep for up to 3 days in the bread bin. After the first day or so, the bread will be better toasted.

Makes 1 loaf (about 20 slices), or 10 small rolls

500g plain white flour, or a combination of white and wholemeal or spelt flour

1 level tsp bicarbonate of soda

½ level tsp fine sea salt

300ml plain, full-fat yoghurt

200ml whole milk

Salt-free oatcakes

Salt-free and fine-textured, these small oatcakes are great as a sustaining snack, and excellent for dipping into mashes or spreads. You can make them with oatmeal alone (use 300g), but combining it with plain flour gives a lighter texture. The fine-textured oatmeal I use here (and in other recipes such as fruit crumbles) should be available from any good healthfood shop.

For babies: Oatcakes are a little bit brittle, so I wouldn't give them to a young baby. Once your baby can chew well, try cutting the dough into small rectangles to make easy-to-hold oat fingers.

For grown-ups and older children: You can add a pinch of salt to the dough, or top the salt-free oatcakes with something flavoursome such as blue cheese and pear, or smoked salmon and horseradish.

PREHEAT the oven to 180°C/gas 4. Lightly grease a large baking sheet, or line it with baking parchment or a non-stick liner.

Put the oatmeal and flour in a bowl and mix thoroughly. Make a well in the centre, pour in the oil, then add enough water to make a firm dough – about 100ml. Knead briefly, just until smooth.

Roll out the dough on a lightly floured surface to a 2–3mm thickness. Cut out small discs (I use a 6cm cookie cutter). Transfer to the baking sheet and bake for about 20 minutes or until very lightly browned.

Leave the oatcakes on the baking sheet for a few minutes, then transfer to a wire rack to cool. Stored in an airtight container, these will keep for at least a week.

Makes 25–30

200g fine oatmeal

100g plain flour

50ml sunflower oil

Spelt & apple stars

These little biscuits have no salt or refined sugar, and they're a nice finger food option for babies who are ready to move on to harder textures. They are also a good alternative to sugary snacks for toddlers – and a fun thing to make with your children. You can create any shapes you like, of course.

FREEZER FRIENDLY

For babies: Try offering these biscuits when your baby's getting the hang of chewing foods such as toast and pasta.

For grown-ups and older children: Serve with cheese or pâté.

PREHEAT the oven to 180°C/gas 4 and grease two baking sheets or line with non-stick liners (or use one baking sheet and bake the biscuits in two batches).

Sift the flours and baking powder together, or blitz briefly in a food processor. Add the butter and rub in with your fingertips, or blitz in the food processor, until completely incorporated. Mix in enough apple juice to make a fairly soft, pastry-like dough (pulsing briefly if using a processor).

Tip the dough onto a lightly floured surface and knead briefly, just enough to bring it together into a smooth lump. Roll out to a 2–3mm thickness. Cut into stars or other shapes, using a cutter, or just slice into chunky fingers with a knife and place on the baking sheets. Bake for about 15 minutes, until just starting to colour.

Leave the biscuits on the baking sheets for a few minutes, then transfer to a wire rack to cool. You can store them in an airtight container for a couple of days, but I think it's best to freeze them and just take a few out of the freezer whenever you need some – they defrost in minutes.

Makes about 30

100g unrefined spelt flour
100g plain white flour, or refined (white) spelt flour
½ tsp baking powder
75g cold unsalted butter, in small cubes
About 75ml apple juice

Quick chick stock

This is a very quick and easy way to make a small quantity of stock, which also produces some lovely, tender poached chicken meat that you can add to all manner of dishes or just serve up plain. This quantity of stock is useful if you're making gravy, or thinning down a purée or sauce. I freeze it, too – it doesn't take long to build up enough for a risotto or soup.

FREEZER FRIENDLY

PUT all the ingredients in a small pan in which they fit quite snugly. Pour over just enough water to cover the meat. Bring to the boil, then reduce the heat and simmer gently for about 10 minutes, or until the chicken is cooked right through (i.e. when the meat is cut open, there should be no trace of blood in the juices that flow out).

Strain the stock into a bowl or plastic tub. Discard the bay leaf. You can discard the veg too, or use them in a soup or purée. The stock and cooked chicken can be used straight away, or left to cool, then refrigerated.

Makes 200–300ml

4–6 boneless, skinless chicken thighs

1 small carrot, sliced

½ onion, roughly chopped

1 celery stalk, roughly chopped

1 bay leaf

Traditional chicken stock

If you roast a chicken – or a couple of pheasants, for that matter – save
the carcasses to make this. You can also often get raw chicken carcasses
(which create a particularly rich and meaty stock) from a butcher. My
local butcher gives them to me for free! They'll probably come without
legs or wings, so use two of them. If your chicken came with giblets, make
sure you add these too (minus the liver).

FREEZER FRIENDLY

BREAK up the carcass(es) with your hands or using
stout scissors and pack into a large saucepan or a
stockpot. Add any other meaty bits or leftover juices, and
the giblets, then the remaining ingredients. You want as
little space as possible left between all the bits and pieces
in the pan, so pack it all down. Pour on enough water to
just cover everything.

Bring to the boil, then turn the heat down low, cover and
leave to cook at a very gentle simmer for about 2 hours.
Taste a little of the liquor and, if it seems good, take off the
heat. If it seems at all watery or weak, remove the lid and
let the stock continue to simmer and reduce to intensify the
flavour. It doesn't really matter how long this takes, just
keep it cooking gently until you're happy with the flavour.
If it's really weak, strain it, then boil it vigorously to reduce
and intensify.

Strain the stock, discarding the carcass(es) and vegetables,
then leave to cool. If a significant layer of fat forms on top,
you can scrape it off, but don't worry if there's just a little.
Once cool, refrigerate for up to 3 days, or freeze.

Makes 750ml–1 litre

1 cooked or 2 raw chicken
carcasses, including any
skin, gristle and leftover
cooking juices (or 2 pheasant
carcasses)

Giblets from the chicken (if
available), minus the liver

2 onions, roughly chopped

2 medium carrots, roughly
chopped

2 celery stalks, roughly
chopped

2 bay leaves

A few whole black
peppercorns

A couple of green leek tops,
roughly sliced (optional)

Vegetable stock

An endlessly useful thing to have in the fridge or freezer, this can be used in soups, risottos, gravies and purées.

FREEZER FRIENDLY

PUT all the ingredients in a large saucepan and pour on 1.2 litres cold water. Bring to the boil, then turn down to a low simmer. Cover the pan and simmer for about 1 hour. Strain out all the vegetables. The stock is now ready to use, or it can be cooled, then chilled or frozen.

Makes about 1 litre

2 large onions, peeled and roughly chopped

2 large celery stalks, trimmed and sliced

1 large carrot, peeled and sliced

1 large leek, trimmed and sliced

3–4 large mushrooms, roughly sliced

1 garlic clove, roughly sliced

2 bay leaves

A few black peppercorns

A few parsley stalks or a couple of thyme stems, if you have them

Baked & flaked fish

This method of cooking fish fillets appears as a step in several recipes in this book – I use it for fishcakes, fish pâtés, fish for pizza toppings etc. I repeat it here because it stands alone as an incredibly quick and simple way to prepare fish for children. I often do white or oily fish in this way, then just serve it up with a few vegetables and perhaps some pasta or oatcakes. I tend to bake more than I need, so I have some left over for another dish. You can cook all sorts of fish like this, but mackerel and chunky fillets of white fish are the ones I usually opt for.

PREHEAT the oven to 190°C/gas 5. Put the fish, skin-side down on a foil-lined baking tray and brush with a little oil. (I use foil here because it makes washing up easier, but you can just put the fish straight on a greased baking tray.) If you like, season the fillets lightly.

Bake in the oven until the fish is cooked through and comes easily away from the skin. For a slender mackerel fillet, this might be 10 minutes, while a really thick, chunky bit of cod could take twice that. It doesn't matter if you have to check it a few times and put it back in the oven.

Once cooked, simply flake the fish off its skin with a knife and fork, carefully removing any bones as you go. Serve straight away, or leave to cool, then refrigerate for a day or two, for use in another recipe.

1–2 adult servings

Fillets from 1 large mackerel or gurnard, or a 200–300g piece of fillet from a large white fish, such as pollack or haddock, or a similar-sized piece of salmon fillet
A little rapeseed or olive oil
Freshly ground black pepper and sea salt (optional)

Polenta 'chips'

Polenta, or cornmeal, is a good alternative carbohydrate if you're bored with rice, pasta and potatoes. It can, though, be awfully bland. My solution is to combine it with stock and a little grated cheese. Cooked until thick, left to set, then sliced and fried, it takes on an appealing new character. If you don't have any stock, just use water – it's almost as good that way.

For babies: These are a nice option for baby-led weaners.

PUT the polenta in a small pan and gradually pour in the stock or water, whisking all the time so lumps do not form. Place over a medium heat and bring slowly to the boil, whisking frequently. The mixture will thicken dramatically and, by the time it's boiling, will be plopping and sputtering away like volcanic mud. Let it do so for about 5 minutes, stirring frequently so it doesn't stick.

Remove from the heat, stir in the Parmesan, and then pour the polenta onto a cold plate (or, if you have one, a marble slab of the kind favoured by pastry cooks). Smooth it into a cake about 1.5cm thick and leave to cool and set.

When the polenta is pretty much cool, slice it into wedges, chips or whatever shapes take your fancy.

Heat a thin layer of oil in a non-stick pan over a medium heat. Add the polenta pieces and fry for several minutes until they form a golden-brown crust on the base. Flip them over and repeat. Alternatively, brush with oil, place on a baking tray and bake at 190°C/gas 5 for 20 minutes or so.

Serve with curries, casseroles or stews, or alongside goujons (see page 137) or meatballs (see burger recipe on page 167), with a salad or vegetable on the side.

3 adult servings, as a side dish

100g quick-cook polenta
500ml chicken or vegetable stock (see pages 236–8) or water
25g Parmesan or other well-flavoured hard cheese, finely grated
Rapeseed or olive oil, for frying

Mini omelette

This is more an egg pancake than a classic omelette, but tempting all the same. I used to give it to my girls when they were very small, cut into strips as finger food. As your child matures, you can add other ingredients, such as finely chopped vegetables and herbs, to the uncooked egg.

For babies: If you're doing baby-led weaning, omelette strips are a good food to try once your baby is used to feeding themselves with fruit and veg.

For grown-ups and older children: Try using the omelette as a wrap, filling it with salad veg or maybe some cold chicken.

HEAT the butter and oil in a non-stick frying pan over a medium heat. Meanwhile, beat the egg lightly, adding the cheese to it if using.

When the butter is foaming gently, pour the egg into the pan, letting it form a roughly round pancake. Let it cook for a couple of minutes, until set on the base and just a bit wet on top, then flip it over and cook for another minute or so until completely set and lightly golden brown.

Serve the omelette straight away, or leave to cool, then cut into strips for babies.

1 adult serving

A tiny nut of butter

About 1 tsp rapeseed or sunflower oil

1 egg

1–2 tsp grated hard cheese (optional)

White bean houmous

You can use the more traditional chickpeas here, but I particularly like the creamy texture of houmous made with white beans such as cannellini. Make sure you use beans which are tinned only in water, with no sugar or salt added. In the summer, this also works well with cooked broad beans – you'll need about 300g.

For babies: Serve spread on toast or oatcakes, or with cucumber sticks. Houmous contains sesame seed paste so it's a food that should be introduced with care (see pages 75–6).

PUT the beans in a food processor. Crush the garlic using a pestle and mortar or the flat blade of a kitchen knife, and scrape about half of it into the processor. Add the tahini, oil, lemon juice and 1 tbsp water and process to a purée. Taste and adjust the flavour with more garlic and lemon juice and, if you like, salt and pepper. Scrape out of the processor into a serving bowl.

You can serve the houmous completely plain, but I think it's much nicer – and more beautiful – finished with a fine dusting of paprika and a little slosh of olive oil. Serve with pitta breads (for home-made, see pages 229–31) and/or raw vegetables for dipping.

4 adult servings, as a dip

400g tin white beans, such as cannellini or butter beans, drained and rinsed

½ garlic clove

1 tbsp tahini (sesame seed paste)

2 tbsp extra virgin olive oil, plus extra to serve

A good squeeze of lemon juice

Freshly ground black pepper and sea salt (optional)

A little sweet smoked paprika, to serve (optional)

Rice pudding

A good old-fashioned nursery pud – soothing and comforting and easy to eat. Delicious just as it is, you can also serve it with raw, stewed or baked fruit, or a fruit purée.

To cook just one or two little rice puds in ramekins, butter the dishes, put 2 tbsp pudding rice and 1–2 tsp sugar in each, then pour in 125ml milk. Add a scrap of vanilla pod to each too, if you have any to hand. Bake for 1 hour, 10 minutes at 150°C/gas 2, stirring halfway through.

For babies: This is a lovely pud for spoon-fed babies who are just moving on from smooth purées, especially if combined with fruit. If you're doing baby-led weaning, put some on a spoon and offer it to your child, or let them eat it with their hands if they prefer.

For grown-ups or older children: Serve with jam, a sprinkling of crunchy demerara sugar, or even maple syrup.

4 adult servings

A little unsalted butter, for greasing

100g pudding rice

65g caster sugar

800ml whole milk

½ vanilla pod, cut in two

PREHEAT the oven to 150°C/gas 2. Butter a shallow ovenproof dish, about 20cm in diameter.

Combine the rice, sugar and milk and pour into the dish (it will look as though there isn't enough rice, but there is). Drop in the vanilla pod pieces. Bake for 1¾ hours, stirring 3 or 4 times during cooking, but leave untouched for the last half hour or so if you want a golden skin to form.

Leave the pudding to cool – just until warm or at room temperature – before serving, fishing out the vanilla pieces as you do so. It's also good chilled (it must be cooled and refrigerated as quickly as possible after cooking).

Variation

Coconut rice pudding For a dairy-free rice pud, grease the dish with sunflower oil. Replace the milk with 400ml coconut milk and 400ml water. This is delicious served chilled (see above) with pieces of fresh nectarine.

OTHER RESOURCES

Breastfeeding support
You might find breastfeeding a breeze, and you may well be offered all the information you need. If not, then get some support. There's a host of organisations who can help, whatever the age of your baby, and they can also offer advice on subjects such as expressing breastmilk and weaning. Try the following:

- La Leche League
www.laleche.org.uk
breastfeeding helpline: 0845 120 2918

- National Childbirth Trust
www.nctpregnancyandbabycare.com
breastfeeding helpline: 0300 330 0771

- Best Beginnings
www.bestbeginnings.info
(includes a good online DVD about breastfeeding)

- The Breastfeeding Network
www.breastfeedingnetwork.org.uk

- Kellymom.com
Very good American site devoted to breastfeeding and parenting

- Lactation Consultants of Great Britain
www.lcgb.org
Lactation consultants may work privately, for the NHS or as volunteers

- Association of Breastfeeding Mothers
www.abm.me.uk
Breastfeeding support hotline:
08444 122 949

- NHS
www.breastfeeding.nhs.uk
NHS breastfeeding helpline:
0300 100 0212

If the first person you speak to isn't helpful, or if the advice you get doesn't seem relevant to you, try someone else.

Further reading

- *Baby-led Weaning*, Gill Rapley and Tracey Murkett, Vermilion
The bible for many baby-led weaners.

- *Child of Mine*, Ellyn Satter, Bull Publishing (US)
Reassuring work from US dietitian who states that the parent is responsible only for providing the right foods at the right time. The rest is up to the child.

- *They are What You Feed Them*, Dr Alex Richardson, Harper Thorsons
Aimed at the parents of children with behavioural problems but relevant to anyone interested in how different nutrients, fats and other substances may affect developing minds and bodies.

- babycentre.co.uk; mumsnet.com
I'm a big fan of the internet forum – a substitute for the extended family or the tribe – and both these parenting sites have good ones. If you ever think your child is the only one who does x, y or z, talking to other parents will probably reassure you that they're not...

ACKNOWLEDGEMENTS

I could not have completed this book without the knowledge and expertise of registered paediatric dietitian Frances Robson. She has worked with me closely on every part of the text, and I am indebted to her – thank you so much Frances for all your hard work. I must also thank Dr Gillian Harris of Birmingham Children's Hospital for her expert opinion, as well as the many other specialists I've spoken to and corresponded with, including nutritionist Judith Wills, speech and language therapist Kate Jones, the American dietitian Ellyn Satter, Joelle Buck of the Food Standards Agency, Janet Clarke from the British Dental Association, Emma Hockridge from the Soil Association and Ruth Beckman of Pesticide Action Network UK.

I am very grateful to all the parents who allowed me to interview them as part of my research. Each and every one of them has added something to this book. Among them are two very dear friends whose additional input and suggestions have helped me more than they know – thank you especially, Emma and Katie. I also owe a great debt of thanks to all the gorgeous children who so graciously agreed to appear in these pages, and to their parents who kindly ferried them to photo shoots.

There are many other talented and hard-working people who have helped to bring this book together and make it look so good. Firstly, a thousand thanks to Georgia Glynn Smith whose delicious photography (and winning way with young models) has brought the book alive, and to the lovely Tabitha Hawkins for her beautiful styling. I am also indebted to everyone who prepared recipes for photography, namely Marina Filippelli, Anna Jones, Gill Meller and the River Cottage kitchen team. And to Natalie Hunt and Richard Atkinson at Bloomsbury, Janet Illsley, Georgia Vaux and Antony Topping, thank you for all your support and hard work behind the scenes.

The River Cottage team have been fantastic, as always. Special thanks go to the wonderful Jess Upton for putting so much work into the photo shoots, to Rob Love for his commitment to the project and to Hugh F-W for all his enthusiasm, encouragement and input.

Most important of all, my love and thanks to the people closest to me, who have supported and inspired me throughout – particularly to my beautiful daughters and my wonderful parents.

INDEX

For Tara, my rose, and Edie, my sunshine

First published in Great Britain 2011

Text copyright © 2011
by Nikki Duffy

Photography copyright © 2011
by Georgia Glynn Smith

A CIP catalogue record for this book
is available from the British Library

ISBN 978 1 4088 0756 9

10 9 8 7 6

The quotation and recipe on
pages 81 and 141 from Judy More's
Teach Yourself: Feeding your Baby
are reproduced by kind permission
of Hodder Education

The moral right of the author has
been asserted

Bloomsbury Publishing Plc
50 Bedford Square
London WC1B 3DP

Bloomsbury is a trademark of
Bloomsbury Publishing Plc

Bloomsbury Publishing, London,
New Delhi, New York and Sydney

Project editor: Janet Illsley
Designer: Georgia Vaux
Photographer: Georgia Glynn Smith
Props stylist: Tabitha Hawkins
Indexer: Hilary Bird

bloomsbury.com/rivercottage
rivercottage.net

Printed and bound in Barcelona by
Tallers Grafics Soler

FSC
www.fsc.org
MIX
Paper from
responsible sources
FSC® C051148

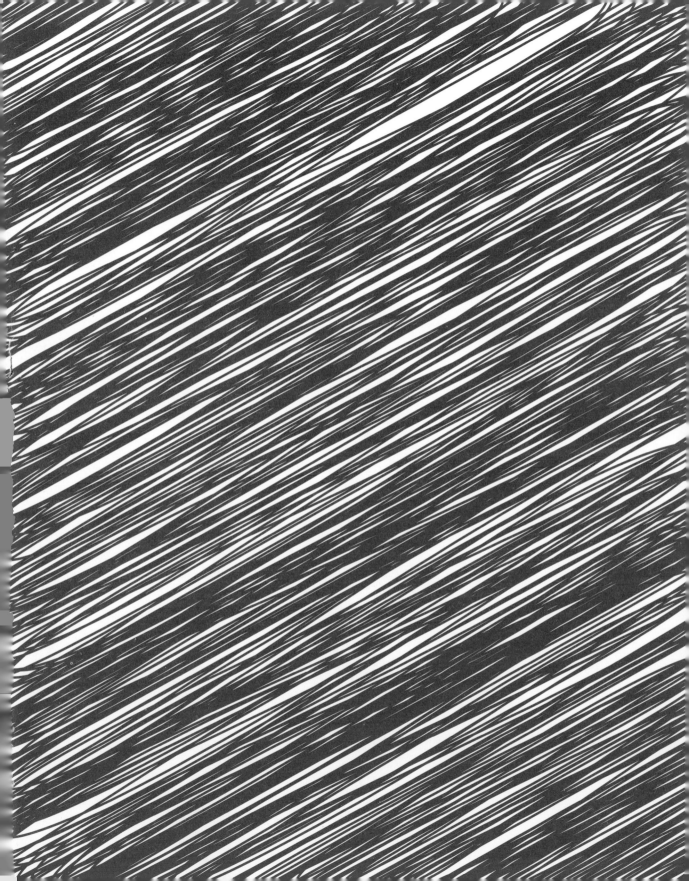

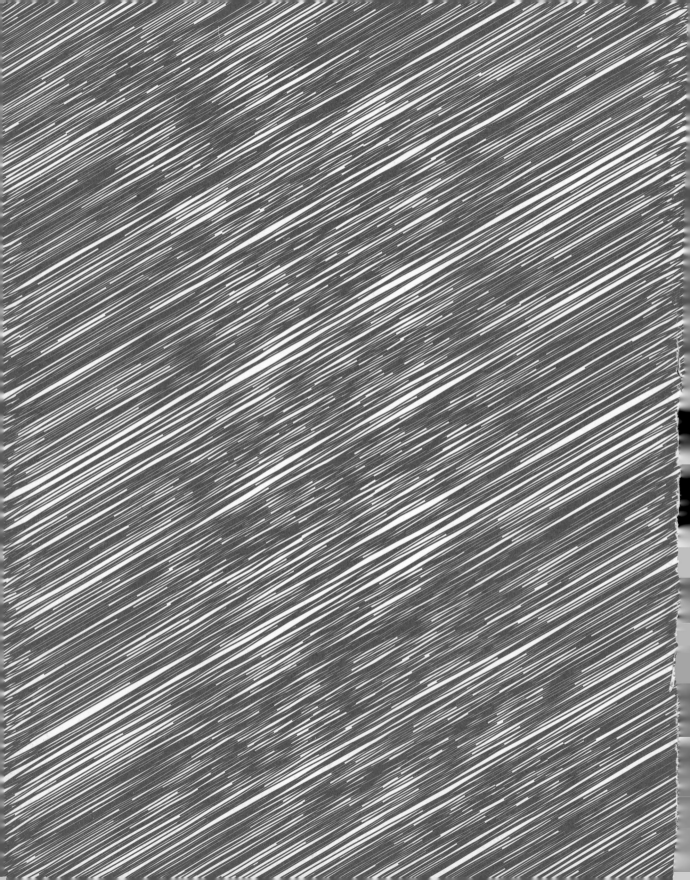